100
WAYS TO STAY SMART
and keep your career on track

ELIZABETH J. CLARK
ELIZABETH F. HOFFLER

BOOK #2 in the
Smart Women Series

StartSmartCareerCenter.org

IOO WAYS TO STAY SMART AND KEEP YOUR CAREER ON TRACK

Copyright © 2016 by Elizabeth J. Clark and Elizabeth F. Hoffler

All rights reserved. This includes the right to reproduce any portion of this book in any form.

Cover design and layout by Martha Rothblum

Printed in the USA

ISBN: 978-0-9908826-2-6
Library of Congress Control Number: 2015916965

CONTENTS

Preface   i

Section 1. Managing Up

Boss Basics	1
Bully Boss	2
How To Work With A Genius Boss	4
Trust In Mentoring	5
Your Boss's Vacation Is No Picnic	6
Feeling Self-Important	8
When Your Best Friend Becomes Your Boss	9
Effective Board Management	11
Asking For, And Receiving, A Raise	13
Professional Generosity Or Professional Stupidity	15

Section 2. Managing Down

Tag—You're It	17
Surprise! All Is Not What You Expected	18
Being A Supervisor May Not Be So Super	20
Value-Based Boss	21
Belief Bending	22
Can You Teach Workplace Anticipation?	24
Words And Wisdom	25
Personal Feelings, Professional Face	27
The Devil Doesn't Need Advocates	29
Charity Conundrum	30

Section 3. Managing Change

Change Is Never Easy	33
Use Workforce Chaos To Your Advantage	35
We've Always Done It This Way	37
Stress Can Be Positive	38
Embrace The Unk Unks	39
The Generational Kaleidoscope	41
If You Can't Afford The Solution	42
Changing Your Team's Force Field	44
Change By Piecemeal Or By Big Picture	45
Dealing With Death In The Workplace	47

Section 4. Leadership Leverage

Don't Postpone Leadership	49
When To Lead And When To Follow	50
Be A Better Leader Than Your Boss	51
Insist On Integrity	53
Value Expertise—Including Your Own	54
Mentors Are Your Secret Weapon	56
Public Disclosure, Personal Harm	57
Reversing A Bad Decision	59
Thought Pioneers	60
Becoming Professionally Humble	62

Section 5. So You're A Grown-Up Now

Giving Up Your Helicopter	65
Your Office Needs To Grow Up, Too	67
Life Insurance? You've Got To Be Kidding	69
Some Conversations Are Harder Than Others	70
What You Don't Know About Your 401(K) Might Be Taxing	72
Who Benefits From Your Benefits?	73
Don't Co-Sign Your Credit Away	75
Be A Student Of Student Loans	76
FICO Fitness	78
Predicting The Unexpected	80

Section 6. Adapting To Life's Changes

Wanting And Having It All May Be Two Different Things	83
Feeling Sandwiched	85
Build A Back-Up Posse	86
Disclosing A Health Issue At Work	88
Private Change Or Public Conversation	90
Don't Postpone Positive Action	91
Preparing To Be A Stay-At-Work Mom	93
Stepping Back In	96
Strategic Job Hopping	97
Too Good To Be True	99

Section 7. Professional Do-Over

Making A Dull Job Shine Again	103
Don't Compound A Career Challenge	105
Refresh Your Résumé	107
Time For A Mentoring Makeover	108

Update Your Personal Brand	109
Shop Your Closet	111
Finding Your Career Center	112
How To Avoid Presentation Arrogance	113
Danger! Opportunity Ahead	115
Own It	117

Section 8. Self-Improvement Never Ends

Inner Strength Inventory	119
You Drive A Hard Bargain	121
Self-Advocacy Is A Required Skill	123
Competitive Edge	125
Be Your Own Cheerleader	127
Your Invisibility Cloak	128
When You Think You're The Smartest Person In The Room	130
Self-Worth Sabotage	132
Discipline Your Calendar	133
Setting Bold Decade Goals	135

Section 9. Business Behavior

Value-Based Work	137
The Go-Along Kid	139
Mentoring Is A Two-Way Street	141
Don't Be A Digital Dinosaur	144
Cast A Wide Net	145
Spinning Time Into Gold At Work	146
Working From Home Might Not Be A Panacea	148
Expense Reimbursement Can Be Expensive	150
Crossing Boundaries	152
Nonprofits Are Still Businesses	153

Section 10. Food For Thought

Forget Failure. Learn From Success	155
The Treasure Of Travel	157
Busyness Is Not A Badge Of Honor	158
Career Paths Are Seldom Linear	160
High Achievers May Not Be The Best Mentors	163
Male-Entrenched Work Cultures	165
Beware Of Self-Proclaimed Experts	167
Being Responsible For You	168
Career Success Is Self-Defined	170
Giving Back	172

PREFACE

ELIZABETH J. CLARK

Our first book, *100 Ways to Start Smart and Get Ahead in Your Career*, was geared towards millennial women who were just beginning their careers, so we were surprised to find it had a much broader audience. One group was women who have been in the professional workforce for five or ten years. They felt the career tips were just as relevant to them as to their younger colleagues. A second group was the mothers of the young women just starting out. They told us they would have found the tips valuable when they were new employees, and they wanted their daughters to have an advantage. They also told us that many of the topics were still helpful to them in their mid-career status.

Perhaps most surprising, and heart-warming, was a conversation overheard between two women in their nineties who had read the book. They had both been employed in professional roles at a time when few women were offered that opportunity. They began their careers during World War II when there was a shortage of men to fill the open positions. They were, in effect, pioneers for all of us who followed. They noted that they had had no one to turn to for professional advice or encouragement, and that they faced many challenges. These challenges increased after the war, when they found themselves in a workforce almost completely dominated by men.

Fast-forward 70 years. Despite the trailblazing efforts of women like these, we have yet to achieve pay or position equity with men. There remains a disproportionate number of men in the higher ranking (and higher paying) jobs, on corporate boards, and in positions of power. Progress has been steady, but not fast enough. Just as the women from the war era, those of us who are well-positioned in our careers have a continuing obligation to assist and support the women who are following in our footsteps.

This second book, *100 Ways to Stay Smart and Keep your Career on Track* is an attempt to do just that. It is meant for the woman who is a rung or two up that career ladder. She may be ready to move out of her first job, to change her position or her place of employment. She may be thinking of returning to school for a graduate or professional degree so that her goals are more attainable. Or she may be entering her first supervisory or management position. The content deals with the difficulties of middle management, where there is a need to manage both up and down. It covers business issues which relate to changes in life status and the fact that planning for the future is simply good business.

The book also emphasizes that continuing education and self-development don't conclude when a woman becomes better established and more confident. Staying current, even ahead of the curve, is required to be ready for the success ahead.

In addition, we highlight the importance of mentoring and supporting women, not just those who are at the first rung of their career, but those who are moving up the career ladder. As soon as you feel ready, we encourage you give freely of your time and expertise. You will find mentoring is a rewarding and educational effort for both of you.

Finally, Elizabeth and I want to thank those women—from a variety of age groups—who suggested topics that needed coverage and who encouraged us to consider a book for the next phase of one's career.

ELIZABETH F. HOFFLER

Writing our first career book *100 Ways to Start Smart and Get Ahead in Your Career* was, in many ways, a reflection of the progression of the relationship between mentor and mentee. I met Betsy when I was a 21-year old intern living in Chicago and she was at the top of her career, leading a national nonprofit organization in Washington, DC. She took a chance on me and I moved to DC to work for her. It was the best decision I've ever made.

We worked side-by-side for over six years, and Betsy taught me nearly every lesson we discussed in the first book. As a young professional, I was extremely fortunate to have found someone early on in my career who was not simply a boss but also a true mentor—helping me navigate daily challenges in the office and pushing me outside of my comfort zone to take advantage of professional opportunities.

Betsy and I no longer work together in the same office, however the lessons learned from our relationship have continued to inform my professional judgment and choices. Our second book *100 Ways to Stay Smart and Keep Your Career on Track* reflects where I am—about a decade into my professional career—and tackles the challenges facing other mid-career professional women. These challenges are a bit more nuanced and complex than those in our first book.

Stay Smart aims to help women find their voice and become comfortable as they take the next step in their careers. When women move up the career ladder, as they become managers and directors, they face new challenges and additional responsibilities. This includes not only figuring out their personal career path, but also becoming a supervisor and mentor to others.

This book will help women to define their goals and take steps to achieve them. We address the components that not only contribute to a successful professional career, but also help women to become leaders. We cover a diverse spectrum of the potential issues that will require women to make difficult decisions. These include personal issues such as family and relationships, health and wellness, and planning for retirement. We also tackle some of the unique challenges that arise in mid-career such as setting boundaries with colleagues, managing change, and deciding on what's next in the career progression.

We hope that readers find this book a helpful compendium to the first one. We enjoyed writing them both, and the positive feedback from women of all ages has reinforced our belief that women have an obligation to support one another as we start smart and stay smart in our careers.

SECTION I
MANAGING UP

Boss Basics

What is it that you want most from your boss? Perhaps the words "praise" or "acknowledgment" come to mind immediately. A salary increase might quickly follow those words.

Almost all of us do better when others recognize our hard work and our efforts. It doesn't have to be a big deal (even though a bonus or raise is great). Sometimes just a simple statement of gratitude from the boss, like, "thank you," or, "nice job," is sufficient. It shows that you made a difference and that what you contributed was noticed and worthwhile.

Other than showing some gratitude or acknowledgment of staff effort, what other traits does an outstanding boss need? Most staff would say that fairness is essential. It is difficult when a boss is unfair in assignments, expectations, or rewards. Giving one employee high profile assignments or exceptional opportunities has a negative impact on other staff and can make it hard for the favored employee to fit in or perform well on team assignments.

Another important trait for bosses is clarity. When you leave your boss's office, you want to know what direction she wants you to take, the desired timeline, and what the expected outcome is. The same is true for your annual performance plan. What are the goals you are expected to reach and how will you be evaluated on the success of those goals?

Many staff find predictability helpful in interacting with their bosses. This especially includes emotional predictability. It is hard to work for a boss who blows hot and cold, who is sometimes easy going, but at other times flies off the handle and is angry and demeaning to staff. It makes work life easier if your boss is predictable enough that you can anticipate her needs and concerns.

These traits—gratitude, fairness, clarity, and predictability—form the four cornerstones of basic (good) boss behavior. Many other individual traits can, and will, be added for each different boss. For example, support, encouragement, kindness, and politeness are all desirable. So are generosity, effectiveness, creativity, and vision. The list is almost endless.

Think for moment about the best boss you know. What is it that sets her or him apart? Notice statements others make when describing this person. Examples might be, "He's tough, but fair." Or, "She always gives credit where it's due." Or, "There are never any surprises with her. She's clear in her expectations."

As you move up the career ladder, these basic boss skills will provide a strong foundation for crafting your own leadership style.

Bully Boss

You can't possibly go through life getting along with every person you meet. If you do, chances are you haven't been passionately pursuing your dreams. We are each a unique composite of talents, quirks, habits, strengths, weaknesses, interests, pet peeves, and idiosyncrasies, which will make some people connect with us immediately. For a variety of reasons, others may instantly find themselves reacting negatively about us. In the scheme of life, it's important to remember that not everyone is going to be our biggest fan, and that is perfectly fine.

However, it becomes a much bigger deal when that person happens to be your boss. Maybe your personalities just don't mesh. Perhaps her vision for your work is completely different than the direction you'd like to go. She might even be taking credit for your work and you don't feel like you can trust her. Issues like competition, jealousy, and pettiness can create deeply complicated working relationships that are frustrating and challenging to navigate.

Unfortunately, in most cases, there is not a lot of recourse, unless you are being harassed or truly bullied in some way. When it's a more nuanced case involving opposing personalities, the bottom line is that the boss calls the shots. Open, honest communication is the best option for reconciliation, but often when you're working for a difficult boss, that approach can fall flat. If it's so bad that you can't tolerate working for a particular person, then it's time to look for another job. Otherwise, you have to "suck it up" and do your best to get along. Chances are your boss is there for a reason and unless you are 100 percent sure that others (in even higher positions) are in agreement with your negative opinion, you need to control your feelings about the situation.

This is one of the trickiest situations any employee can face on the job. If you allow yourself to be locked into a miserable situation, it can destroy your mental health and wreak havoc on your job performance. Navigate these treacherous waters maturely, avoid burning bridges, and exit gracefully when it's time to go. Sinking to her level will only harm your reputation and result in regret.

How To Work With A Genius Boss

Many very smart people rise to the level of boss, and if you are lucky, you work for one of them. Sometimes, however, you find yourself reporting to someone who is super smart. The pace at which they think, the connections and conclusions they draw, and the creativity they express can be hard to follow and impossible to emulate. They may always be two or more steps ahead of where you are in your thinking about an issue or in your planning. These bosses can be fun and exciting to watch in action, and you can learn a tremendous amount from them.

Sometimes, however, they can be terrible bosses. Because they work so quickly, they feel employees take too long to finish a task or to arrive at a conclusion. Or they can be like a sparkler, sending out a hundred ideas all at once for you and the team to try to sort through and manage. They may not see value in sequential efforts, preferring to experiment with several different approaches at the same time. That adds immeasurably to the work load.

These super smart bosses also may easily be able to stay on top of the literature and developments in the field. In fact, they probably write some of it. They may have a memory like a steel trap. Some may actually have photographic memories.

Sometimes bosses in this category have workplace eccentricities. They can be highly competitive and treat every discussion like a scientific debate. They may be impatient and they "don't suffer fools gladly." They may get distracted easily and work exceedingly long hours trying to understand a small point or solving a problem not particularly relevant to the issue or crisis at hand. They can have tunnel vision. They may not pay attention to office protocol or office politics. Perhaps they have no time for things that others, including their own bosses, feel are important.

How do you work effectively with this type of boss. First, be open to the way they work. Recognize that you won't change them or their work habits. Anticipate their needs when you can. Help them with details and with things they don't have time—or wish—to do. Never try to con them or pretend that you know or understand something you don't. Ask thoughtful questions. Be genuinely interested. Observe how they think and problem-solve. Don't take their impatience or criticism personally, and recognize that probably no one can measure up to their high intellectual standards. Learn what you can, which may be a great deal, and take that experience and knowledge with you when you move on to your next job.

Trust In Mentoring

Whether your mentor is outside your organization or whether it's a senior colleague at your workplace, a mentoring relationship requires mutual trust. First, there has to be a clear willingness to engage in a mentoring process, both for the mentor and the mentee. You each should be fully committed to the endeavor and be clear about the goals, expectations, and limitations.

Both mentor and mentee need to trust that the discussions during a mentoring session or exchange will be kept confidential. The mentee may be experiencing a brief lack of confidence or a workplace conflict that could have the potential to be damaging to their career if the situation were disclosed. Similarly, the mentor may use a past personal or professional example to help make a point, but might not want that example to be common knowledge. Disclosing sensitive or potentially embarrassing information to others compromises trust and can quickly derail the mentoring relationship.

The mentee should also be able to feel confident that the mentor is working in their best interest. There should be no competition or concern that ideas or work of the mentee will be attributed to the mentor. The mentoring relationship should never feel coercive or overly directive. The goal is for the mentee to learn from the experience of the mentor, not to be managed by the mentor. A mentor should help the mentee consider possibilities, but the final decision about problem resolution or career advancement must rest with the mentee. Despite the career success and greater experience of the mentor, a mentoring relationship is based on collegiality, not on status or a power differential.

Additionally, a mentoring relationship must be based on honesty. If the mentee can't trust that the mentor is being completely honest, that the mentor is sugarcoating the issue or making a situation sound better (or worse) than it is, confidence in the process will be lost. Likewise, if the mentee withholds pertinent information or gives a skewed version of a situation, the mentor not only will be at a disadvantage, but may begin to distrust the mentee's integrity or ability.

While the setting and the purpose may differ, the mentoring relationship is not unlike other important personal relationships. To be successful, it requires support, honesty, integrity, and trust. If any of these elements is missing, the relationship will be ineffective and short-lived.

Your Boss's Vacation Is No Picnic

You may know the drill. Your boss is going on vacation. She feels the office doesn't run well when she is out and she is trying to cover all the bases before she leaves. This includes short deadlines and speeding up projects. Or she begins delegating additional tasks to be done while she is gone. Your to-do list is overflowing.

As much as you may look forward to her being out of the office for a while, you dread the before and after period. The first few days after she returns may be even worse than the days before she leaves. She wants updates on everything. She is certain projects couldn't have run smoothly without her scrutiny and input. As a result, she seems to be in a state of chaos for a day or two. She comes in like a tornado, and it takes a certain amount of time for the commotion to die down, for things to settle and get back to normal.

How can you manage these uncomfortable periods? First, remain calm. Don't add to her discomfort. Next, try to anticipate her needs and concerns. Then take the initiative. Make your own list of things that will have to be done in her absence. Give her a copy of the list and ask what else you should focus on while she is out. Ask her if she would like to receive any email or texts while she is absent.

Be sure you have an update report ready and on her desk when she returns. If there were any problems, highlight the issue, but also include what has been done so far to remedy the situation.

Most importantly, keep in mind that the boss's vacation does not mean you and your coworkers can also take an in-office vacation. Yes, the boundaries may loosen a bit, and coworkers may seem more relaxed. There may be fewer meetings and less performance pressure, but that should not translate to less work getting done or fewer hours spent in the office. It's often a good time to catch up with tasks that you previously haven't had time to finish. Most importantly, be sure to complete all of the items on the list that you told your boss you would cover while she was out.

If things run smoothly when your boss is on vacation, she may feel less worried the next time. Or she may simply be a person who likes to control things and will always feel frantic before and after a planned absence. Either way, with some preparation, you have the opportunity to show your boss that you can function well both when she is in the office and when she is out.

Feeling Self-Important

You've been an outstanding employee. You work hard—harder than many of your colleagues. You're a team player and you often end up directing the project at hand. You have great institutional memory and you are a creative problem-solver. You may even be the boss's right hand.

However, your exceptionalism is not always noted. For example, you discover that all of you in a certain rank got the very same bonus amount this year. That seems unfair to you because some of your colleagues do the bare minimum day after day. Worse yet, you just learned that the newest hire is making a bit more than you are. That is not only unfair, but infuriating.

Soon, you find yourself becoming self-focused. You begin keeping score of who does what and who achieves more. You begin feeling resentful and used. You question going the extra mile or pitching in. You go from being a model employee to an apathetic one.

You begin thinking about confronting your boss, even issuing an ultimatum. Either your salary is raised to equal or exceed that of the new hire, or you will leave. You think about how difficult it would be to replace you, what a big hole your leaving would make. You even wonder how long it would take the organization to recover if you left suddenly.

There is probably no bigger mistake you can make than issuing an ultimatum to your boss. In many ways, an ultimatum gives a boss little choice. They can't allow themselves to be bullied by an employee, even a really good one. If you threaten to resign they, more than likely, will accept your resignation.

Instead, ask your boss for input on your performance and what it will require to move to the next level or to get a salary increase. Do not mention the new hire (you shouldn't know her salary anyway). Don't whine or boast. Listen carefully to her response. If she doesn't see your value or you are really at a dead end in your current job, you may need to consider other options. However, give yourself some time to think about the conversation, and don't do anything hasty. Good jobs are hard to find.

Also, think a bit about self-worth versus self-importance. Did you feel you were valued before you learned about the uniform bonuses or the salary of your new colleague? In the past, have you been treated fairly, even recognized? Can you see a career path or a way to move forward?

If you can answer these questions positively, maybe your high opinion of yourself is getting in your way.

If you do decide to stay, consider whether or not you can recover your energy for, and commitment to, your job. There is nothing worse than feeling resentful every day. Eventually, you will hate coming to work, and your attitude will undermine and erode your hard-earned reputation.

There are times to take a firm stand about equal pay for equal work. There may even be times when you do leave a job because of inequities. But if and when you do, do it on your own terms and for the right reasons. Self-importance is not one of the right reasons.

When Your Best Friend Becomes Your Boss

You and your best friend have worked side-by-side for several years. You make a great team, and you trust and support one another, both in and outside of work. Recently, your manager decided to retire and your best friend was asked to replace her. All of a sudden, your best friend is your boss.

You know your friendship is strong. As a result, you should be capable of having an open discussion about the change.

You recognize that her work role will be different while yours will remain much the same. You understand there will be management issues, including personnel decisions like salaries and disciplinary actions, that can't be disclosed. As two friends who are used to talking about all things work-related, it will be important to clearly define the new boundaries.

There are several land mines to be especially aware of when friendship roles change. First, there will be a power differential. Due to her job, your best friend now gets to make decisions about work assignments, vacation approvals, and, perhaps, even your salary increases and bonuses. Even more difficult is the fact that your friend will be responsible for your annual evaluation.

Perceptions of others about your friendship might also take on new meaning. Will your coworkers think you now have an unfair advantage or special privileges? Will your friend—now manager—worry about the same thing and go to extremes not to show favoritism? If so, will you start to feel abused and disadvantaged?

Depending on the specifics of your job and the strength and longevity of your friendship, you may both settle into the new work relationship with relative ease. You may be thrilled she was promoted and you want to help your friend succeed in her new position. You're able to handle the new challenges, and your work day and your friendship continue much like before.

Sometimes, however, it simply becomes too awkward. You know each other's strengths, weaknesses, and preferences. You know each other's lives including personal issues, even secrets. That makes the task of being in a subordinate role especially difficult.

If you find yourself struggling, try to have a direct conversation with your friend. Or perhaps someone in human resources could be a confidential sounding board. Don't make any hasty decisions, and give things a chance to settle down. If after your best effort, the work arrangement simply isn't working, it might be time to start looking for another opportunity at work, or to consider making a lateral transfer to another unit. The goal is to keep your job as well as your friend.

Effective Board Management

If you work for a nonprofit organization or agency, you probably are familiar with a volunteer board of directors. Boards are required as part of the nonprofit governance structure. They have several essential functions. Most notably, they provide strategic direction, and ensure the mission of the agency or organization is achieved. They have fiduciary oversight to be certain monies are used and accounted for correctly. They also hire and evaluate the CEO or Executive Director.

Board members have varying levels of expertise, experience, and expectations. Sometimes, they mistakenly think they have daily administrative or decision-making roles, or they think the CEO is simply a staff person to do their bidding. These are not accurate perceptions, and they can quickly derail the board-staff relationship.

If part of your job description includes a governance function or board management, familiarize yourself with the duties and role of a nonprofit board. It is helpful to prepare and conduct new board member training sessions and to have job descriptions for board officers and board members-at-large. This sets the parameters for your partnership and helps to define your complementary, but different, functions.

Boards need adequate and accurate information to do their job. It's up to the CEO and staff to provide this information in an understandable format and in a timely manner. Never withhold information from a board member or tell them something untrue or so vague that you are purposely clouding the issues or misleading them. At the same time, do not discuss sensitive personnel issues or disclose personal information about staff or clients unless it is essential to the work of the board or there is a legal reason to do so. Then, only do so in executive session where the board is aware of their commitment to confidentiality.

Being gracious and accommodating towards board members goes a long way. Remember that they are volunteering their time to help your organization or agency.

At the same time, it is best to avoid friendships or personal relationships with board members. This is especially true if you are in the chief executive role. If you are the CEO, the board will set the components of your contract, determine your salary structure, and complete your annual evaluation. That means there is always a power differential. In effect, the Board Chair is the boss of the CEO or the Executive Director.

If you hold a staff position other than the CEO, be certain that you always apprise your boss of any interactions with board members or any requests, especially any from the Chair of the Board. Be certain you are always discreet. Never complain about the office or your colleagues and never reveal unnecessary or confidential information. Perhaps most importantly, never try to use a board member to circumvent a decision your boss has made. Similarly, do not try to gain power by attempting to garner the support of a board member or two. This almost always backfires.

Board management is a skill set. By understanding the role of boards, and by observation of, and interaction with various boards of directors, you can become expert at board-staff relations. As your career progresses, you may find yourself in a volunteer board position. When you do, your experience from the staff side will serve you well.

Asking For, And Receiving, A Raise

There is nothing quite as nerve wracking as asking for a raise, but there is a way to reduce your anxiety and prepare a best-case scenario for yourself.

Before you even begin your job, you should do several important things to ensure that you're beginning at the salary you deserve. First, you should research what others in similar positions are making. This is fairly easy to do with plenty of resources available, particularly through online career services. You can also chat with people in your industry and if you have a close and open relationship, you can inquire about their salary range. Next, you should negotiate your starting salary based on this range. Never accept the first offer or you risk leaving money on the table. During the hiring process, you can also ask about the raise and promotion structure to fully understand how the organization operates. There may be a specific process in place, or each employee may be responsible for her own career progression.

After you've been in your position for some time, you can consider asking for a raise. Self-advocacy is key. You have to believe that you are doing an exceptional job and that your hard work deserves additional compensation. However, you can't assume that your boss will easily recognize all of your contributions because she is busy, and you are probably one of many employees she supervises. Even if you have a great relationship with your supervisor, it's important to be prepared with a list of your specific accomplishments and how they contributed to the overall success of the organization. Create an outline with your biggest projects or major responsibilities and underneath each, detail the initial goals and how you exceeded expectations. This should include the specific impact you had on multiple aspects of the projects. Use metrics wherever possible to illustrate your value.

Keep in mind that persuasion is critical. Know what is important to your boss and align your message with those values. You should also know what approach is most likely to elicit a positive response from your supervisor. Does she prefer conversations to be quick and to the point or does small talk before a request help to put her at ease? Treat your raise request like any other workplace conversation but keep your end goal in mind. Most importantly, don't ever be hostile or negative, regardless of the direction or outcome of the conversation. Keep the conversation positive and focused on you. Don't compare yourself to others or invoke ultimatums.

Timing is also important. Don't expect a raise six months after you've been hired. Enough time must pass in order for you to make a significant impact worthy of a raise. The one-year mark is a good milestone to begin thinking about what you've accomplished and preparing your pitch. If your annual review is approaching, prepare your pitch prior to that discussion. If you are taking on new responsibilities, that is also an opportune moment to request a salary increase in line with your expanded duties.

If you receive the raise you've asked for, you have to plan your next steps. How can you build on your past success and create even more value for your organization? A promotion may be your next goal, so determine if that is a possibility and how you can reach the next level. If you weren't successful in acquiring a higher salary, ask for suggestions or performance criteria to improve your performance and ultimately receive the salary you believe you're worth.

Professional Generosity Or Professional Stupidity

In the workplace, there are generalists and specialists. For example, your formal expertise may be in communications or marketing, grant writing or fundraising, clinical care or management. Some of these skill sets overlap, and you may have expertise in more than one category.

A problem can arise when you are recognized as having a broad skill set, especially if you have skills that others in the workplace lack. For example, you grew up using technology and you are good at both trouble shooting and computer applications. You found that many older office staff were struggling with computer issues, and they began asking you for assistance.

Also, many staff—even higher level staff—do a poor job when writing or editing. Because you are known as an excellent writer, others have come to you to review or edit their reports or speeches.

At first, it was flattering. Eventually, though, you began to see that others were taking advantage of your professional generosity. You now find yourself staying late or working at home in the evening to finish colleagues' assignments. You even find yourself scrambling to meet your own commitments and deadlines. You are angry at yourself and feel you have been naïve, perhaps even stupid.

Several of the people you routinely help are in higher level positions. You don't report to them, but they tend to ask for your assistance fairly regularly. You are uncertain about how to refuse or how to extricate yourself from all of the extra work. You don't want to offend them or cause difficulty for your boss.

There are several approaches you can use. Begin by turning down a request for something that isn't too critical or time sensitive. Simply apologize and explain that you are too backed up to take on an extra assignment right now. Better yet, offer to show the appropriate assistant (that is, their own assistant) how to complete the task so that they will be able to help them going forward.

Before you are asked for assistance the next time, write out easy and clear instructions for how they can create their own presentation or format their document. Tell them you will be happy to briefly help them if they get stuck.

If none of these suggestions seems to work, you may need to have a conversation with your boss. Explain the situation. Mention that you were only trying to be helpful, but that the work you are now being asked to do for others is interfering with your own workload. Ask her for advice or if she could intercede on your behalf. You might suggest hiring a temporary staff person or securing a contract editor or graphic designer so there is consistency and so that well-written and well-edited reports and presentations can be produced.

Even if your boss speaks with her colleagues, you still may find some of them quietly asking you for a favor or disregarding what has been asked. It will be important to hold firm when this happens. If pressed, you can respond that you will have to get your boss's approval first. That will probably help curtail future requests.

It's a positive thing to be a team player and to be willing to help others in the workplace. It's also fairly easy to find yourself stuck in a situation where others begin taking advantage of you. When that occurs, it's critical to extricate yourself from the extra work without alienating colleagues.

SECTION 2
MANAGING DOWN

Tag—You're It

A promotion to management is an exciting opportunity. Perhaps you have been trying for some time to move up at your current place of employment. Maybe you opted to apply for a higher level position at another organization and have been notified that you were chosen for the job. Or there has been some restructuring and reorganization at work, and you were taken by surprise when your boss told you that you are being promoted to a supervisory position.

Sometimes you have a few weeks to make the transition, but other times, you begin your new role with only a few days' notice. You recognize that the initial meeting with your future staff is important for setting the tone of your management style going forward, but you may not yet be totally certain about what that style or philosophy is. Of course, you have some ideas, but they likely aren't fully formed yet.

There are some basic guidelines that can be helpful. You may not be able to control the timing or structure of the initial meeting with your new staff, but you can control how you present yourself. Before the meeting, spend time thinking about and crafting your introductory remarks. Be certain you don't sound boastful, or self-effacing, or defensive. The goal is to be gracious and confident. Do not disclose too much personal information, and recognize that it is too early to lay out your vision for the future. There will be plenty of time for that once you have gotten a better lay of the land.

If you are now going to supervise colleagues who were your coworkers, the meeting can be even more challenging. These individuals already know you. Perhaps they think you are the best choice for the position, or they may secretly, or even openly, question your selection or your ability to be their supervisor. Again, remaining non-defensive is your best option. You should stress how much you value their support, and that you look forward to continuing to work as a team.

Beginnings are important. Do your best to start off on the right foot as you climb that ladder.

Surprise! All Is Not What You Expected

When you begin a new job, you have to make numerous adjustments. You need to quickly learn the organization's culture. You also might benefit by researching its history. Why was it started? What was its purpose then compared to its stated purpose now? You hope you will fit in well and that your goals align with those of the organization.

Sometimes, it takes a while to settle in and be accepted. Sometimes you are disappointed that there aren't more employees your age or with interests similar to yours. Or perhaps you were looking forward to working with the people who interviewed you, and soon after you begin, there is a reorganization and you are assigned to a new team. Or maybe the person you thought would be your boss gets promoted or leaves shortly after you start.

No matter how much research you did before accepting a job, there can be surprises. People and organizations change. A place of employment may have to adjust to economic factors, and some benefits might change. That great 401(k) employer match you were impressed by may be reduced. Or the amount you have to pay for health insurance will increase at the start of the new fiscal year.

How you manage surprises in a new workplace will partially determine how successful you will be in your job there. You certainly have the right to ask some questions, but keep in mind that you are only one employee, and that the organization has an obligation to many and their loyalty won't be to you, the newest employee. You may find that management was equally surprised by your boss leaving to accept a new position, or they were hoping the year would end with a better financial position.

The best thing you can do is to be adaptable. The worst thing you can do is quit abruptly. There is nothing to be gained by walking out in a fit of anger.

You can express disappointment, but do so professionally. Don't make any threats, or statements that could be misconstrued as threats. Never give an ultimatum (such as I don't think I can stay if I can't work with someone as talented as Bob). Frequently, statements like that are met with an offer to accept your resignation.

Keep in mind that you don't want to be unemployed and remember that unemployment insurance is not available to you if you quit. Also, remind yourself of the time and effort it took for you to find your new job. Do you really want to start over right now?

Instead, remain positive. Do not engage in office gossip or office politics. Do not complain to coworkers. You have dealt with setbacks and organizational surprises before, and there is frequently great opportunity when things are unsettled.

Determine some timelines and milestones for assessment. Wait three months and see how you like your new boss and how well you are fitting in with your team. At six months, determine if the job has growth potential and if you feel you are learning new skills or are being offered new opportunities. At a year, take a look at the salary and benefit situation. If the organization is still in financial crisis and more cuts are probable, it might be time to update your résumé and get serious about looking for something new.

Being A Supervisor May Not Be So Super

Most employees want to move up the career ladder at work. Perhaps you look at your own supervisor and wonder how hard her job could really be. You may feel you could easily do her work and do it better than she does.

Supervision requires a specific skill set, yet the needed skills usually are not taught in the classroom nor in the workplace. Employees who do an outstanding job in their clinical or direct practice positions are often picked for a supervisory role despite a lack of expertise in supervision. Being a supervisor may, or may not, be a good fit.

Supervision carries with it a variety of personnel functions—preparing schedules, approving leave time, dealing with staff complaints, and evaluating employees who report directly to you. It may also have a budgeting and/or financial function.

As a way to begin, you need to become familiar with, and closely follow, policy guidelines for your organization. You also need to be aware of legal mandates such as making accommodations for an employee with a medical need, issues of pay equity, and dealing with interpersonal conflicts like sexual harassment, hostile work environment, and gender or age discrimination.

Managing your staff in a fair and impartial way is essential. This can be difficult if your promotion means that you are now supervising coworkers, especially those with whom you are friendly or have social relationships. Likewise, staff evaluations can become challenging, doubly so if you get to determine individual staff salary increases.

If only cursory on-the-job training is available to you when you become a supervisor, seek out a trusted colleague at a similar level and ask her to help guide you through the pitfalls. If you need to do budgeting, take an online course or see what is available in adult education at your local community college. If personnel issues are tricky, seek guidance from your own supervisor and/or the company human resources department at the first sign of trouble.

You may find that you have great people skills and that you love being a supervisor. Or you may find you dislike managing staff and personnel problems. If this is the case, keep an eye out for a position like project or product management or grant writing that doesn't require your being responsible for staff oversight. Supervision is only one path to the top. You may prefer a different route.

Value-Based Boss

Being a supervisor or boss comes with perks—a bigger paycheck, more autonomy, greater prestige, and the fulfillment that comes from coaching a team to success. However, along with those perks also come new responsibilities. While it is in your purview to make sure that your staff are performing to the best of their ability, that also means that you have to help them get there.

Some employees require little hand holding, come in on time, stay on task, and perform at the level that you expect of them. However, they are few and far between. Others require a bit more cheerleading.

They need to feel valued. A simple "thanks" may not suffice when they've submitted an assignment that they've worked particularly hard on. They might respond best with pointed, supportive feedback. This doesn't mean false compliments, but it does mean encouragement and positivity when it's warranted, and helpful and constructive criticism.

Managing staff can get overwhelming. Additional responsibilities can mean added pressure. Juggling a packed schedule can result in unintentionally neglecting the daily details but that doesn't mean you can let your staff down. They are your strongest resource and when they perform well it means that you are leading them well. However, it requires consistent, predictable, honest feedback and support. You may not even realize that you are taking them for granted, especially when they are performing well. Remember, though, that they are looking to you for guidance and approval. If you are rushing around, responding tersely to emails, and canceling weekly staff meetings, it can easily and negatively impact your staff's morale. Simple, daily reminders to staff that they are valuable contributors to the overall mission of the organization can be the best investment you make in their well being and growth as an employee.

Belief Bending

We all arrive at adulthood with some things we believe as absolute truths and firm rules. Some of these we learned from our families. Perhaps some were learned in religious training or in educational programs. For example, you may believe all people are basically good, and that forgiveness is a virtue. You may believe that everyone deserves a second chance, or you may think some actions are so egregious that there is no recovery from them. Similarly, you may or may not believe people can change or can be rehabilitated.

You carry these beliefs into your work setting where they may not always match the philosophy of top management, your boss, or your human resources Department. For example, you may think everyone makes mistakes and should be given a second chance. Your organization, however, may be concerned with possible litigation and is quick to dismiss someone who makes a serious error.

In addition to major beliefs, there can also be minor differences that create discomfort for you as a manager. You may see punctuality as an important employee attribute, but your organization offers a flexible start time. You know some staff take unfair advantage of this perk, but it is difficult to document or manage without appearing punitive. Or there may be a system in place whereby there are only two or three reasons—stealing, insubordination, workplace intimidation or violence—where an employee can be fired outright. Other issues, such as job performance, repeated tardiness, or unexcused absences, require a staged approach where the employee has the opportunity to improve time after time, and you find this tedious and non-productive.

Many talented individuals get ahead in their careers because they follow the rules. They do what is required and asked, often going beyond the basics. In so doing, they may become rule bound and have little tolerance for employees who cut corners or constantly try to bend the rules. If you fall in this category, you might wish to take a firmer stand than that which is acceptable in your organization. This can create issues for you.

Becoming a manager often requires a reassessment of what you believe are black and white workplace issues. Start by checking the employee policy manual, and then talk with a representative from human resources. Get advice at the first sign of difficulty with an employee. It would undermine your credibility to go down a disciplinary path and find out that management can't, or won't, support you.

As you become a more seasoned manager, you will learn several important lessons. You will find that there are many, many grey areas in the workplace. These will challenge your thinking and sometimes even cause you to temper your belief system a bit. You also will discover that some things that initially seemed important to you simply aren't worth your time and energy.

Can You Teach Workplace Anticipation?

If you've moved into management at a fairly rapid clip, you probably have the skill of workplace anticipation. It starts with good observation skills. You watch your boss and your colleagues. You study how they work, how they behave, and how they interact with their peers and with their superiors.

More than likely, you have spent time learning the habits, the likes and dislikes, and the needs of your boss. You know how much discussion about a project or issue is enough, and how much is too much. You know how to write the perfect summary memo, and how to net it out verbally. You recognize when more research is needed and what type and format of data are preferred. In short, you have great anticipation skills.

An employee who can anticipate is a valuable asset. For the boss, the anticipator saves time, serves as a sounding board, and as a fact-finder and fact-checker. In return, the employee has not only the ear, but the trust, of their boss.

Fast forward. Your anticipation skills paid off, and you're now a new boss. You feel swamped with details and decisions. You need your staff to step up, to take some initiative. You find yourself feeling disappointed again and again. Why can't they be more on top of things and better understand what you want from them?

If you find yourself in this situation, stop and take stock. Make a list of what you need and what your preferences are. Do you prefer staff communicate with you electronically, or do you prefer hard copy, or both? Do you need the first or last hour of the day to be free of meetings so you can catch up? Is it important to you that meetings start on time and end on time, and do you want a written meeting agenda in advance? Is there a format you prefer for summary reports? Do misspellings and errors in grammar make you crazy? Do you want to be kept in the loop on every detail or do you value independence in your staff? Most importantly, what do you need them to anticipate?

Once you have completed your preference list, go over it with your staff. Lay out your ground rules, and then stick to them. When an employee is late for a meeting, call her on it. If a report comes in with typos, send it back and ask that it be corrected and resubmitted. Tell an employee when an email is unnecessary, when a report is too long or disjointed, or when a meeting did not serve a purpose.

Savvy staff will take note of your preferences and will match their habits and actions to yours. They will become familiar with your requests and expectations and become more adept and confident in meeting your needs. One or two of them will become indispensable. Unfortunately, they are the same employees who will quickly move up that career ladder—just like you did.

Words And Wisdom

Words have power, both positive and negative. They can be curses, blessings, oaths, and threats. When arranged in a certain way, they can be poetry. Many words strung together on a page or on a screen can turn into a great piece of literature or a boring report.

We applaud good speeches and laugh at the comic's routine or a funny joke. We can be dazzled by good hype and put off by vulgarity. Words can make us feel distant or embraced. They can convey kindness or bitterness, respect or disdain. Even the absence of words can speak volumes which is why therapists warn us against "the violence of silence."

One of the unique characteristics of words is that they evoke feelings. They can make us happy or sad, angry or proud. We celebrate the first words a child speaks, and we cherish the words of a dying loved one. Words even have the power to give or take away hope. When mixed with great emotion, words can live in our memory forever. For example, the words, "Will you marry me?" or, "I want a divorce!" have an emotional impact that can last a lifetime.

In the workplace, as in life, praise, or words of encouragement, can carry us a long way. In contrast, harsh criticism or words spoken in anger can defeat us. If you work in a stressful situation, with a boss who flies off the handle or shouts insults when something goes wrong, your colleagues may suggest that you simply need to "grow a thicker skin." They tell you not to let the boss's tirades affect you personally, that the issue will pass. That is so much easier said than done.

You have now moved up the career ladder. Perhaps you have changed positions or even changed organizations. You have a new boss and you now have staff who report directly to you. As a result, the words you use in the workplace have become even more important. They have more power because you have more power.

Based on your past experience, you are determined to be a fair, respectful, and supportive boss, not a jerk like the one you previously had. You know you want to encourage your staff, not belittle them. You also will give credit where credit is due, and you will not blame others for your mistakes in judgment.

You learned the hard way that how you talk to others and the tone that you use can be just as significant as what you actually say. You have promised yourself that, as a manager, you will never raise your voice, or shout, or swear at employees. You also will not freeze out staff by ignoring them because they disappointed you. In short, you will be a better boss than that miserable person who previously held some sway over you.

So, always choose your words carefully and be respectful—whether speaking to staff, colleagues, or your boss, especially your boss. The words, "You're fired," are words you never want to hear, even if spoken quietly and kindly.

Personal Feelings, Professional Face

Some people have "poker faces" and others generally can't tell what they are thinking. Other individuals are more open and what they are thinking is easily determined by their facial expressions. When you know someone well, you may be able to read their unspoken feelings. For example, you probably know when your mother is displeased even if she doesn't speak a word. You can tell when your best friend is hiding something or when your sibling isn't being completely honest.

When you move into a management position, you need to think more about what you say and how you interact with those you supervise. As the leader, you are no longer "just one of the girls." If you are responsible for assignments and evaluations, you will need to create a bit of distance to accommodate the power differential that now exists. When in management, you also have an obligation to maintain the party line and to see that certain tasks are completed and directions followed. Your personal feelings may need to take a backseat to professional edict. Individuals in middle management roles often feel conflicted. They now have an obligation to upper management, but may still identify with line staff. This can be a recipe for career disaster.

There are several things you need to avoid. First, you must never speak against management decisions when interacting with staff. You can't give an order and say that you disagree with the issue or idea, but you have no choice in the matter. This is like playing two sides of the field. If you disagree with a proposal or directive, express your opinion and make your argument at the management meeting. Once a final decision has been made, it is up to you, as a manager, to own and support it.

Second, don't make exceptions for staff because you disagree with a directive. Exceptions have a tendency to backfire, and staff may believe that they can count on you to always take their side or to see their position when, in fact, you can't.

Third, don't express negative opinions about your own boss or others at the top. This includes when speaking with other managers, close colleagues, or the staff who report to you. You agreed to be part of the management team, and you owe them respect and loyalty.

Fourth, never disclose confidential information you have obtained by being a part of management. This again applies to all of your internal work relationships (including your closest work colleague) as well as externally. Discussing private business matters with outsiders could result in a professional reprimand or even dismissal from your position.

Finally, practice managing your facial expressions and your tone of voice. Before meeting with your staff think carefully about what and how much you will say about a new directive or business decision. Decide how you will handle queries or challenges, even anger, from staff. Keep in mind that anyone can be recording your words on their cell phone, and that misspoken words may quickly come back to haunt you in unexpected ways.

It can be difficult to transition from being one of the gang to being one of the bosses. Moving up the career ladder requires a higher level of awareness. Despite your personal feelings, you always want to present your professional face.

The Devil Doesn't Need Advocates

We've all been there. The meeting has dragged on and on. It looks like the team has finally arrived at an action plan. Things are winding down, tasks are being assigned, and you are ready to pack up and get back to your real work. At that very moment, someone says, "Let me play devil's advocate" and launches into a rehash of the previous discussion. Colleagues groan inwardly, everyone hoping the boss will dismiss this unnecessary showmanship.

The concept of "devil's advocate" has its roots in the Roman Catholic Church. It was the title of the person appointed to challenge a proposed canonization or the verification of a miracle. Today, the term is defined as a person who argues a position, not because they are committed to their argument, but because they wish to extend the debate or continue the discussion.

Why do some employees feel the need to do this? If they have an opinion, or concern, why wasn't it offered during the general discussion? Instead they sit there like the Sphinx, waiting to undo hours of debate and planning just as it is coming to a conclusion. Sometimes they even withhold a critical piece of information to use as leverage when they finally claim the floor.

Most workplaces spend a great deal of time in lengthy (and often unnecessary) meetings. In addition, not all managers are adept at running efficient meetings or making quick and firm decisions. Other workplaces have a highly competitive environment where dissent and conflict are tolerated, perhaps even encouraged. These types of workplaces are prone to devil advocacy.

So, how can this behavior be avoided? First of all, promise yourself that never, under any circumstance, will you personally use such a lame ploy. If you are the boss, refuse to tolerate this maneuver for getting attention and trying to show up others. If you are the team leader or group facilitator, when you go over the ground rules for the meeting, include "no playing devil's advocate" as one of the firm rules. And, if you have a coworker who has a penchant for grandstanding as a devil's advocate, send him or her a copy of this chapter.

Charity Conundrum

Some employees love being involved with charities and participating in community events. Perhaps they were raised in a family that felt volunteerism was an important civic duty. Or community service was required as part of their high school or college curriculum, and they found they liked being a volunteer and assisting organizations to achieve their fundraising and program goals.

Other employees may not be as interested or involved, or they may want to keep their support of various charities or groups private. Additionally, the community where the workplace is located may not be the community where many employees live, and they may prefer to participate more locally or give to a cause closer to home. Still others may feel they lack either the time or financial resources to take part.

It's a good idea for organizations to have clear policies about hosting programs or holding fundraising events at work. Without a policy, these efforts can get bothersome, and one person's cause may be offensive to others. It may seem benign to ask colleagues to buy Girl Scout cookies or to support a son's little league team, but other causes can be more partisan. Most of the time, though, asking others for financial contributions simply creates an awkwardness among coworkers.

In addition, if you are the supervisor or boss, it is never a good idea to ask employees to support a favorite cause of yours. No matter how much you declare that it is voluntary, employees may still feel an unfair pressure to give or participate.

A more acceptable approach may be for your organization to buy a table at a fundraising gala or to make a financial contribution to a community event. This is usually covered by the marketing budget and is a mechanism to garner community awareness of the company or its products. It has a business, rather than a personal, purpose.

Many corporations do encourage community involvement and they may set aside a day or a certain amount of hours for employees to engage in volunteerism. Some do this on National Volunteer Week or National Make a Difference Day or at some other specified time each year. Once again, this needs to be a personal decision and choice for each employee and not a thinly veiled attempt to get publicity for your organization.

Many individuals see community service and fundraising for a good cause as positive things. In the workplace, however, what begins with good intentions can end with bad feelings.

SECTION 3
MANAGING CHANGE

Change Is Never Easy

Each workplace has a life of its own. It has structure and function. It has a history and a narrative, and it goes through various developmental phases. It has a reputation and a social standing among like organizations. It also has a unique social and psychological environment.

Most importantly, an organization has a specific culture. Large organizations also have numerous subcultures. It is the organizational culture that shapes workplace behavior and determines how the organization makes sense and sets norms, and how and when things are done. Cultures, by definition, must be dynamic, but most cultures are difficult to change, and usually they only change in small increments. They generally resist change, and often the culture regresses to its former state at the earliest opportunity.

If you are a new boss, especially if you were hired from the outside, don't begin with mandating big changes. Take time to observe the culture of the organization or your new unit. Your success as a leader will depend, at least partially, on how well you understand it. As a boss or supervisor, you can control many aspects of your unit or organization, but it is almost impossible to control culture. Culture is largely determined and controlled by the group, not by the leader.

There generally is no one "correct" organizational culture and not all aspects of an existing culture will be important in bringing about needed change. Some cultures, however, are unhealthy. A culture of fear (fear of bosses, of being bullied, or belittled, or fired) is one such example. A culture of mistrust is another one, as is a culture of apathy or of corruption.

So, as the new boss, how do you start? It's almost always a mistake to begin by quickly reorganizing or by immediately bringing in your own staff. A better first step is to meet with all of your managers or lead staff. Then meet with employee groups. Ask your peers about the existing culture. Take some time to observe carefully and to develop the most comprehensive understanding of the existing culture that you can. Then develop a clear vision of where you want to take the organization and what change will be needed. When your vision is set, you are then ready to determine your change strategies and your timeline. It is essential to incorporate relevant aspects of culture change at every step of your change process.

Inexperienced bosses often underestimate the impact organizational culture can have, and how it can impede needed change in the workplace. Even strong leaders can be defeated by strong cultures. As a new manager, make certain you view culture as a worthy opponent and prepare your strategies accordingly.

Use Workplace Chaos To Your Advantage

You may love meeting people, traveling to new places, and taking exotic vacations. You may enjoy special activities and assignments at work or attending business events and conferences. If someone asked you how you feel about change, you might say you welcome it, that you like to see things from a different perspective. You might even say that change helps you grow and keeps you from being bored. All of that could be true. Yet when it comes to big changes in the workplace, many—if not most—of us resist change.

As employees, we become accustomed to, and protective of, the ways we do things. We usually take the same route or mode of public transportation to work, park in the same area, eat meals at the same time, and watch the same tv shows. We stick with favorite brands and eat favorite foods. Routines are predictable and safe.

Knowing your job requirements and how to work with and please your boss are also important considerations. So what happens when major change is announced? Perhaps there is going to be a corporate reorganization or a flattening of departments with fewer managers overall. Or management has decided that all staff are moving to a different location, maybe even a different city or state. Or a new strategic plan has been adopted that phases out, or transitions, your department or position.

This magnitude of change has a tendency to induce personal and professional panic, and if leaders are not well trained to manage change, temporary chaos can result. Employees may start sending out résumés or lobbying for new positions. With a situation like this, what is the best path for you?

First of all, try to remain calm. Learn all you can about the change without snooping or resorting to gossip. In meetings, ask respectful questions. Try to assess if the change will have a significant impact on you, or your department, or your manager. Look at the potential opportunities and possibilities for growth.

Do not be openly critical of the decision or the decision-makers. Recognize that you don't have all the facts and may never have all the facts. Don't try to get colleagues to divulge confidential information and don't divulge any yourself no matter how tempting.

Be careful with your interactions with management. Don't make threats or statements that you can't work with someone, or that you won't report to a certain individual. You never know where your name will appear on the organization chart when the dust settles.

Don't sulk, or be overtly negative, or be passive aggressive. Don't call in sick or take unofficial days off as payback. Don't start coming in late or leaving early. Don't try to skirt assignments and don't undermine your colleagues or your boss.

Instead, think about how you can help manage the change. Finish outstanding assignments, make notes, and develop plans necessary for the transition. Volunteer information when needed and be a team player. Your boss may have her hands full with a thousand problems and details. Determine how you can be most useful.

You may not end up with the department, boss, title, or assignment that you were hoping to get. But, if you have done your research and have done your part in managing your personal and departmental chaos, you will still be a step ahead of your colleagues who did nothing but criticize and sabotage.

We've Always Done It This Way

Organizations and corporations can get stuck. Perhaps the same boss or management team has been in place for years—even decades. The procedures manual hasn't been updated because everyone "knows how things are done around here." Maybe computer systems, human resources policies, and marketing efforts haven't kept pace with current practices, yet, coworkers seem comfortable, even complacent, and not interested in rocking the boat.

If you find yourself in such a workplace, what are your options? If a static environment isn't what you are looking for, how can you help your team or your organization move forward? Are your only choices finding a new position or giving in to inertia?

It may be difficult to bring about positive change in a "stuck" organization, but there is also great opportunity if ideas are presented in thoughtful, non-threatening ways, and if management can be shown the return on their investment. Occasionally, a system just blows up and a new fix is essential, but, more often than not, needed change in a conservative workplace will have to be incremental.

Nothing seems more arrogant than a new manager or new employee, impatient to prove her or himself, quickly suggesting that things could be done differently, and in a better or more efficient way. It seems like an affront to the established worker who may have helped to develop the current system or procedure in the first place.

The most important step in bringing about change is to carefully and thoroughly assess the situation. Why has something always been done the same way? What are the stumbling blocks and why is change resisted? Is there a champion or ally for the needed change in the management ranks? Is there a critical mass of interested employees who can work together for the change?

Think for a moment about why people generally resist change. They resist change they don't understand. They resist change that is forced upon them. They resist change when they aren't a part of planning for it. Recognizing these barriers can be helpful when you are trying to lay the groundwork for moving an idea or a change effort forward.

Being a workplace change agent requires both skill and foresight. It may also require patience and perseverance. Keep at it. You were hired for your expertise and ideas, not for maintaining the status quo. Keep an open mind yourself, and if coworkers bring ideas to you, resist ever using the excuse that "we've always done it this way."

Stress Can Be Positive

Years ago, endocrinologist Hans Selye differentiated stress from eustress. Eustress was defined as the good stress, the kind of stress that motivates and challenges you. Today, we hardly ever read about eustress. Instead, there is an entire billion dollar, anti-stress industry that tells us how to relax, do yoga, meditate—all worthwhile activities, but many people thrive on stress. These individuals are not necessarily adrenaline junkies, nor do they have any interest in extreme risk. They may simply like success and winning. Stress may help them achieve more and at a higher level, or help them face challenges and find the best way forward. It may help them think faster and move to action more quickly.

If you aren't good at managing stress, the following might be helpful suggestions. First, become an expert on your own personal stress. Be able to differentiate good stress from bad stress. What types of stress motivate and excite you? How do you use stress in your life? How do you manage stress?

Then, pay attention to your stress triggers. Be aware of what is causing you negative stress. Is it a lack of time, financial difficulties, relationship problems, or work issues? When you realize that not every problem causes you stress, you may be able to isolate your main stressors and begin to transform them into challenges that can be overcome.

Think about what constitutes an ideal stress balance for you and work towards that. Unless you are on vacation, a complete lack of stress is probably not desirable. At the same time, being overscheduled and overloaded to the point of feeling frantic is also a negative.

Look for meaning in your stress. Are you working for an important cause or doing valuable and significant work, or is your current stress a necessary step toward a future goal? Keep in mind that stress can be a resource that helps you achieve at a higher level.

Finally, recognize your stress tipping point. Even people who love stress can reach the point of stress overload. We all have a stress capacity limited by our physical and emotional resources. Recognize when you are getting close to your limit and get some rest, relief, or assistance.

Embrace The Unk Unks

It's easy to say no. It takes up far less time and energy to take the easy way out. It may even be human nature to try to avoid the difficult, time consuming, challenging choices. However, very little is truly impossible. More importantly, you will never meet your potential or create something important by immediately refusing to take on big tasks and daunting projects. Think about it—what are your big picture goals or your personal moonshot? You won't get there by being the person who always has an excuse.

Think back to your first job. It's a good bet you rarely said "no" to assignments. Perhaps you were afraid to push back, but more likely, you simply did not know what you did not know, and that meant that you dove in without hesitation. This phenomenon is referred to as the "unknown unknowns" or the "unk unks." Unk unks are a source that should be tapped into more often. When we don't know what we don't know, we aren't afraid to take risks.

Here are some prime opportunities to embrace the unk unks. When you are facing a new task and these excuses pop into your mind, channel the unk unks:

"I don't have time to do it."

There is plenty of time to accomplish big things. It comes down to priorities. If you embrace the unk unks, you can fit new things into your to-do list, but you won't judge how time and energy consuming they might be.

"We don't have the resources to do it."

This might be legitimate but it's also an easy go-to excuse when you don't want to do something. You shouldn't get in over your head, however there is usually a way to find the resources necessary to get worthwhile things done.

"We don't have the capacity to do it."

Like time, there is always capacity, it's just a matter of priority. Reassess what is important, rearrange urgency, and reassign staff to make the capacity.

Most of these issues come down to either fear or laziness. Neither should drive your career.

Next time you are making a decision about whether to take on a project, don't immediately go through your mental list of why it's impossible. Think back to a time when you were less cynical, frustrated, or burned out. Clear your mind, embrace the unk unks, and see what happens.

The Generational Kaleidoscope

Multigenerational workforces are like the glass in a kaleidoscope. The distinct pieces eventually blend together and form changing patterns.

Each generation has an historical perspective which will have an impact on the workplace. Many people who lived through the Depression of the 1930s were left with a memory of mass unemployment which translated into a strong work ethic and loyalty to the corporation where they worked for most of their lives. Or perhaps workers your grandparents' age were college students during the protest era of the Vietnam War. That experience may have formed their activist personalities, and they may be favorable towards unions, believe in equity, and are willing to question authority.

Generational differences are at play at all multigenerational workplaces. For example, that boss in his seventies views things through a certain lens. He believes work is central to life (it is to his), and everything should revolve around it. Additionally, he may not trust new things, so he is slow to embrace something as nebulous as the Cloud.

Or, your departmental director might be your parents' age, and she holds beliefs about work habits and professional dress similar to those of your mother. Her generation didn't grow up with computers and smart phones and constant connection. You find her approach to problem-solving slower or more deliberate than what you prefer. She assumes assignments will take longer than they do and seems suspect if you get done quickly. (Remember your mom and your homework?)

Your direct supervisor may be in her thirties and in the midst of raising young children. Her work day requires rigid structure. She has to leave on time because of child care, and she needs you to match her work schedule or to tie up all the loose ends. She knows there is a better software out there, but she simply doesn't have time to learn to use it.

You may find it difficult, even tedious, to respond to so many work styles and constraints. Regardless, don't assume you have nothing to learn from the various generations. Many things, like ethics, business principles, and market forces, are still relevant. You also can gain a vast knowledge of your area of interest simply by listening and trying to determine what from the past helped to shape your field today.

At the same time, you may wonder when those ahead of you will begin to understand the generational imprint of your own age group. No one is suggesting going back to handwritten bookkeeping or to typewriters, but you feel the tug backwards every work day. What you may not realize is that those in leadership positions are also feeling the tug of your generation to move forward.

You probably won't have much luck in quickly changing the mindsets or the work behaviors of those who have been in the workforce for years. However, you and your peers can, and will, have an impact on the future. As more of you are hired and promoted, you will start to bend that generational curve, and the kaleidoscope will turn once again.

If You Can't Afford The Solution

There's an ad in airline magazines that says, "If you can't afford the solution, it's not the solution." While the ad is touting the services of some company, the advice is germane to many organizational issues. When tasked with finding a solution to a thorny and repeating problem, employees may develop optimal, even elegant, plans only to watch them get shot down as soon as the boss sees the price tag. When that happens, they might feel embarrassed that they didn't realize the financial parameters, or they may feel angry that they expended so much effort and wasted a lot of time.

If it's a repeating problem, numerous other people probably have tried to fix it over the years with little lasting success. Too frequently, the answer is fairly obvious, but the resources or talent are not available to actually correct the situation. This results in a band-aid approach where the problem is patched temporarily, most likely to occur again at a critical time.

When you find yourself facing such a situation, start by doing some good organizational research. Talk to people who have been there for a while. If you can find them, talk to the staff who have actually attempted to fix the problem in the past. Read any reports and proposals you can find. Do a timeline of the previous efforts and an analysis of why it wasn't successful. In doing so, you may actually find an innovative way of approaching the current situation.

In some cases, you might find that the actual problem is much bigger than you thought or people realize. This isn't necessarily bad. Understanding the total scope of the problem may lead you in a new direction or point you to a more innovative path.

Also ask the boss for some budget parameters. If she is thinking $10,000 and you are working with a proposal at five, or even ten, times that amount, your solution, as the ad says, will not be the solution.

If cost is the limiting factor, consider breaking the proposal into several time chunks, perhaps spanning budget years. Or check to see if there are some creative options such as applying for community or grant monies to help offset the cost.

Early small successes in solving the problem go a long way. Try to be certain that completing stage one will actually result in some positive change. If people can see any improvement in the overall problem, there may be more motivation to keep the correction process moving forward.

Finally, steer clear of naysayers, people who tell you that others have tried and failed, and that you will fail, too. Some organizational problems do seem intractable, yet we know all problems can be solved. By using good historical research, budget parameters, careful planning, and by adding your own creativity and enthusiasm, you may find you are the one who will find the solution after all.

Changing Your Team's Force Field

You've been part of a work team for several months. They call you a team, but you're a team in name only. Instead of working together, there is backstabbing and undermining. Some team members dislike one another and take opposing sides on issues just for the sake of argument. It takes a long time to move forward, and many tasks get stalled.

The supervisor is ineffective, and has been unable to manage the team. Now she is going on leave for three months and you have been assigned to the role of interim team leader. It wasn't a request, so you had no opportunity to think about whether or not you wanted this particular assignment. The question now is how can you move the team from negative to positive?

The first important step is to assess your own past team behavior. Have you contributed to the team's problems, or have you tried to be a peace keeper or moderator? Have you blended in with the woodwork, and tried to work independently, or have you been a cheerleader or major contributor?

Being a team leader requires both good communication and good negotiation skills. Assignments and timelines must be clearly defined. Each member must be held accountable, and the team, as a group, must be held accountable. It's often useful to record the goals, tasks, and deadlines for the project. It's an even better idea to post them in a spot where everyone, including the unit manager, can see the progress.

There also have to be team ground rules. If these were previously set, but are no longer used, set them again. Modify what hasn't worked, and add new rules as needed. When someone violates one of them, like being hostile or coming late or missing meetings, address the behavior immediately. Use the group's power—like team peer pressure—to keep people in line and focused on the tasks, not on the personalities.

You might also appeal to team pride. If team members realize that management considers them a dysfunctional team, they might begin to realize that they are personally being "painted with the same brush." Team failures often have personal consequences.

Some successful projects do get done by teams that are not particularly team-like, but it takes more time and energy. In addition, poorly operating teams are the major reason many staff dislike being part of a team in the first place. On the other hand, highly functional teams, such as a surgical team in an operating room, a champion sports team, or a flight crew during an emergency, are evidence of how valuable teamwork can be.

With some effort, excellent communication, clarity, support and encouragement, you can help your negative team become a positive force.

Change By Piecemeal Or By Big Picture

When you begin a new job or position as a supervisor or team leader, many colleagues will have advice for you. Your new boss will give you some direction, and the previous title holder might leave a notebook of important information for your use. Your colleagues generally will be quick to tell you what they think should be done with your department or unit. More than likely, they will also feel free to tell you about your staff—the achievers, the laggards, the golden girl, and the boss's niece or nephew.

You can learn a great deal from unsolicited input and personal opinion, but don't take it as fact and don't immediately act on it. Instead, try and suspend judgment and store the information away to consider when you have a bigger and better picture.

If you repeatedly hear negatives about one employee, you may want to take extra time to review past annual evaluations and even speak with human resources. Check to see if the current situation or lack of success is a relatively new phenomenon. Perhaps she was recently promoted and hasn't had the necessary training or support she has needed. Or maybe she has missed quite a lot of worktime due to an illness or family crisis. Underachievers often shine when a new supervisor takes over.

Some suggestions about needed change in your departmental operations may sound helpful. Store these away for later, too. New bosses can make the mistake of trying to bring about change too quickly. If you put changes in place and find that they don't work or were misinformed from the beginning, you appear inexperienced at best, and inept at worst.

Perhaps you have been promoted from within. You have felt for some time that the unit has been mismanaged and you welcome the chance to finally correct things. If this is the situation, slow down immediately. Keep in mind that you only know some of the facts, and that your own perceptions and beliefs, even your culture, may color those. Seek the clarification of others and allow for the possibility that you might be viewing things in a biased way.

Once you have completed a thorough assessment, you have carefully evaluated your team and all available data, and have learned what you can, it will then be the time to put all the pieces of the workplace puzzle together. When you have the big picture, you'll be able to see which pieces are missing or are misfits. That is the point when planned change should begin.

Dealing With Death In The Workplace

When a work colleague dies, it often sends the office into a tailspin. If the death is sudden and unexpected, the response may be even greater. The whole workforce may be shocked and overwhelmed by the news.

There are several steps to take when this happens. The first is to provide adequate and accurate information about the situation. People will naturally be curious and concerned. It might be helpful to call the staff together for the announcement. At that time, inform staff about what management plans to do—send flowers, send a delegation to the funeral, start a fund for the family.

At the same time, if you know them, review the family's wishes. Will there be a private burial or is it appropriate for staff to attend? If staff can attend, will they be given time off to go?

While it may seem insensitive, you will also have to quickly decide who will take over, at least temporarily, the work functions for which the deceased had responsibility. Phone calls and emails also will have to be transferred.

Other than that, it is usually better to let some time pass before taking down name signs, or cleaning out the office. This allows colleagues an opportunity to adjust somewhat to the loss and the change.

Some deaths are particularly difficult to handle. These include situations such as an employee dying while in the office, or an employee committing suicide. For these types of situations, it is helpful to have a grief counselor speak with the staff as a group, or make individual counseling available.

Other losses are more hidden and personal, but not less important. Fetal loss is one example. Having a miscarriage is traumatic, and frequently, no one knows what to say or do. The employee probably won't want any public acknowledgment of the loss, but notes from others are almost always appropriate. An unrecognized loss creates an increased grief burden for the person experiencing the loss.

As a society, we are death avoiding, and many people are uncomfortable with grief. We don't know what to say or do when someone dies. Even if you never need it, it's important to have a policy and a plan in place for handling death in the workplace. While it won't alleviate the feelings of sadness and grief, it will provide some stability and comfort.

SECTION 4
LEADERSHIP LEVERAGE

Don't Postpone Leadership

You are sitting in a staff meeting and the team is struggling with putting a plan together. You have excellent project management skills and you've always been a leader. It would be easy to stand up, map out the project on the white board, and make assignments. But you don't. Your supervisor (who is not a particularly strong leader) is in charge of the meeting, and you know she wouldn't appreciate your riding in for the rescue. Your colleagues keep glancing at you, hoping you will, once again, get them out of this morass.

You make a few strategic and careful comments, and you encourage others to chime in. Slowly, though, you become the focal point. Your leadership skills have popped up again, despite your trying to downplay them so your supervisor won't think you are trying to upstage her.

It's hard to hide your leadership ability. It's also tedious, and it's a waste of time. You were a leader at age five when teams needed to be organized on the playground. You were a leader in grade six when you were elected class president.

When did it become necessary to tone down your capabilities, to make others think you were less of a leader? Too often this happens in middle school when girls back away from competing with boys in their class. Someone may have labeled them "Little Miss Know-it-All," or the teacher might have admonished them to "give others a chance to answer." The message may have been blatant or subtle, but it was the same message—girls shouldn't be too visible, they shouldn't be leaders.

Now that you're a grown-up (and a professional), take a look around. Do you actually think men ever worry about taking a leadership role? Or are they in the middle of the discussion or debate trying to get their viewpoint across, even disregarding the voice and ideas of others, sometimes including their boss?

As a leader, you do want to be considerate, inclusive, and collaborative. You do not want to upset your boss. You do not want to hog the spotlight or muscle your way into the discussion, but you shouldn't be sitting there waiting to be invited in either. You are a leader. Accept that fact and lead.

When To Lead And When To Follow

We often see children playing "follow the leader." It's an age-old game that small children seem to enjoy. What's most interesting is who gets to be the leader and how those decisions get made. Every now and then, an individual is described as a "born" leader, but, generally, if a person wants to be an outstanding leader, leadership skills have to be learned, practiced, applied, refined, and used again and again.

Some work situations require leadership. Some even demand it.

There are, however, times when your leadership is not expected nor even warranted. Some of these situations include when you lack the actual knowledge to assume the leadership role, or when there is someone obviously more qualified to be the leader. You don't want the leadership role when it's actually a dump job or it's work that no one really cares about. You certainly don't want to assume the leader role if you think you are being set up for failure by a colleague or a competitor. Finally, you shouldn't assume a leadership role if you are already so overloaded with current commitments that you can't possibly absorb, or do justice to, one more project.

That's not to suggest that you shouldn't volunteer for leadership situations. Being a successful project or team leader is a good way to get recognized by your boss and the administration. Failing in a leadership role also gets you noticed, but in a negative way.

So, instead of being like the child who always raises her or his hand to be in the front of the line whenever "follow the leader" is suggested, try and choose your leadership opportunities carefully. You can always participate as a good team member. Sometimes, however, it's better to follow the leader than be one.

Be A Better Leader Than Your Boss

Many people think that being a boss means being a leader. While it's true that bosses have power, get to give direction, and tell people what to do, that doesn't necessarily make them a leader.

On the other hand, many leaders never become a boss. In fact, some prefer not to be in that position.

If you're just starting your professional career, you may be wondering who wouldn't want to be the boss. They make more money, they have a staff, they have perks, and they get to make decisions. All of that is true, but that still doesn't make them a leader.

What, then, are the qualities and skills of a leader? Is it something innate—do you have to be born a leader—or can you learn leadership?

Some people do seem to show leadership skills at an early age. We see this in school athletics, in student government, on debate teams, and in community service activities. Other people, as they gain education and experience, seem to grow into the leadership role.

What skills does it take to be a leader? Equally important, how can you best hone your skills so that your leadership potential is noticed?

One of the most critical leadership skills is the ability to listen to others—especially to those with opinions and suggestions different from yours. Leaders realize they can't, and don't, know everything and that the input of colleagues and staff can be key to solving a problem or turning a situation around.

Another attribute of a leader is the ability to maintain momentum and enthusiasm. This skill can be seen frequently during sports events, where the actual leader of the team is someone other than the team captain. This is just as common in the workplace where you find a staff member, other than the boss or manager, encouraging colleagues to try harder and finding solutions to what seem like unsolvable problems.

You also find that a leader frequently sees opportunity in set-backs. That's not to suggest that you adopt a "Pollyanna" attitude (which only irritates your colleagues), but be certain you don't become a "naysayer," quickly vetoing the solutions and ideas of others. Look instead for patterns and synthesis in their suggestions. Can they be tied together in a creative way? Can the group move forward without having all the answers?

One final attribute of leadership is teamwork. Leaders don't quickly take individual credit, but are quick to point out that it was a team effort.

Make it a habit to pay attention to the skills and qualities of the individuals who are the formal or informal leaders in your organization. Note what attributes they display, how they listen to and motivate others, how they voice their opinions, how they problem-solve, how they lead. Then practice what you have observed and work to develop a personal leadership style others will notice and admire.

Insist On Integrity

Integrity should be at the core of any professional's personal mission. Integrity is tied closely to character, and both have been described as doing what is "right" even when no one is looking. It would make sense that people who are drawn to nonprofit careers would be imbued with a strong sense of integrity, but, unfortunately, this isn't always the case.

First and foremost, integrity should drive your decisions at all times. Most of the time this is simply a matter of common sense. If you know something is wrong, such as stealing, lying, cheating, or just cutting corners in general, don't do it. Don't embellish your résumé or lie about how much money you make. Don't sneak out of work early without accounting for your time. Don't submit personal receipts for reimbursement. Don't gossip about others in the workplace or trash your employer once you move onto another job.

Insisting on integrity becomes more challenging when your colleagues or boss don't seem to have the same values. If your boss is the CEO and is lacking integrity, it is probably time to find a new job. Cases of questionable integrity aren't typically obvious or cut and dry. You probably will not have to deal with someone embezzling money and committing fraud, but chances are there will be decisions that you question. In the heat of the moment, it's easy to tell white lies or exaggerate progress. Perhaps a deadline is approaching and someone makes an excuse that isn't quite true in order to buy more time. Someone may take credit for another person's work. Maybe a colleague plagiarizes and passes it off as original content.

It's important that you speak up when you do not agree. It is wise to refrain from confrontation and to calmly and clearly explain why something makes you uncomfortable. If the issue in question is potentially illegal, extract yourself from the situation and go through the proper channels to report the action or behavior. It only takes one instance of lapsed integrity to seriously jeopardize your career.

Value Expertise—Including Your Own

The internet and its extensions like Facebook, Twitter, Instagram, and texting have made it simple and easy to be in contact with a large number of friends, colleagues, and strangers. We now have consumer reporters and bloggers who give their views on almost every subject. We also have websites developed specifically to inform us about issues like our health care or how to find a reputable service. As a result, it is difficult to identify real expertise from personal opinion, conjecture, and marketing.

Perhaps nowhere is this more evident than in health care. You develop a new problem or symptom and you research the issue online. You find a great deal of advice, much of it conflicting. One site recommends nutritional supplements, another recommends over-the-counter medications, and yet another suggests exercise. Once you have sifted through all the information, you arrive at a self-diagnosis, which may or may not be correct. On the negative side, you put off getting an expert opinion from a qualified health care professional. You may also miss the opportunity to prevent your condition from worsening, or you may actually make it worse by following the wrong advice.

There are many areas, in addition to health care, that can have equally disastrous results. How to manage or invest your money, how to deal with legal issues, how to deal with work problems or relationship situations come readily to mind.

Doing research online can be helpful and informative. Considering it as expert opinion is not. Asking for advice from your network of friends and colleagues can be useful, but accepting their consensus as expert opinion is not.

Life problems do not equate with computer problems or with finding a plumber or electrician. When you need to make an important decision, turn to trusted and recognized experts for advice. Online advice does not equal seeing a physician, an attorney, a mental health counselor, or a financial adviser.

In addition, advice you receive online or from friends or colleagues can make you question your own opinions. You may begin doubting your decisions or questioning your feelings or options. Perhaps friends think you should quit your lousy job or accept that new position across the country. Others suggest dumping your unemployed partner or buying that luxury item. Still others may discourage you from returning to school or changing careers.

When it comes to your life, no one is more expert than you are. You can seek input from others, but make sure the big decisions are your own. You—not your friends, nor work colleagues, nor someone you have never even met—are the person who has to live with the outcome.

Mentors Are Your Secret Weapon

Mentors come in many different forms and they serve a variety of roles. If you participated in organized athletics in high school or college, your coach, in addition to helping you achieve on the playing field, may have served as a role model and mentor. Perhaps he or she encouraged you to look at a certain college program and wrote a letter of reference for your admission.

College professors, especially those in your major concentration, often fill mentoring roles. Maybe one or two of yours were helpful when you were trying to find the right path through all the available choices in your chosen field. These were the professors who offered, or agreed, to write letters of reference for your job application or for graduate school.

As a professional, you may have to work a little harder to find a mentor. Many people are happy to give you advice, but a mentor goes beyond that. They are interested in you achieving and succeeding at the highest possible level. They are accessible and keep confidences. They support and encourage you, without imposing their personal views or goals. They are usually in a background role, in fact, they often are outside your place of employment. Their success doesn't depend on your success.

Can bosses be mentors? Some can, but it's tricky. They can be excellent role models, but because there is a power differential—they hold your paycheck after all—it may be a bit of a conflict. It also can be difficult to talk to the boss you are trying to impress about your insecurities or future career hopes and goals.

Can your circle of friends serve the mentoring role for you? Some researchers have noted that young people today don't value expert opinion. Instead they look to a consensus of opinions from their peer network. It is always helpful to have the support and encouragement of your friends, but generally, your friends are no more experienced than you are in employment matters. That's where a mentor comes in.

Mentors generally have years of experience upon which they base their advice. They have acquired a certain wisdom in your field and for your situation. They can help you think through situations and consider options. They encourage you to take a risk, confront an issue, try a new approach, and find a positive resolution to your problem or situation. You can rely on them to be thoughtful and non-judgmental.

Mentorships can occur spontaneously or more formally. Someone may introduce you to a person you simply click with and with whom you want to continue the conversation. Or you may eventually approach someone in your field and ask them for career advice. If you find a person willing to become your mentor, make it a point to keep the relationship going. Keep in touch on a regular basis. Let them know you value their support and input.

Mentors are like a secret weapon for workplace success. If, during your career, you have one or two or more, consider yourself very lucky.

Public Disclosure, Personal Harm

What loyalty do you owe your company, or your boss, or your work colleagues? Are you obligated to publicly defend work policies or products? What information can you divulge and what cannot be made public?

In this era of over-disclosure, many people post personally revealing items for public view. They tweet trivia without great thought or self-censorship. This sometimes results in blurring the line between personal information you own and information that actually belongs to your employer.

If you work in a company that develops products and has patents, you may have been asked to sign an employee non-disclosure form when you were hired. If you have an employee contract, there may be a clause that states you agree not to work for a competitor for a specified period of time when you leave the company or finish your consulting work. When you sign one of these, it becomes a legal document, and you can be sued for breech of contract for disclosing trade secrets.

If you are employed in a health care setting, there are strict laws that protect the privacy of patients and clients. Even inadvertent disclosure can result in your being fired or sued. Many health professionals also hold licenses that can be suspended if they fail to maintain professional ethical standards.

Confidential work data such as personnel records, departmental budgets, organizational audits, contracts, or business proposals are the property of your employer. You are not free to provide them to friends working on a similar project, or to make and keep copies of them for your own future use. Even if you contributed to writing a grant or developing a program or product, they are considered "work-for-hire." You were paid for your efforts and you do not have ownership.

If you decide to write an article about a case or a work project for publication in a trade journal, be certain to get sign-off from your employer before submitting it for editorial review. Likewise, if you are asked to give an interview about a company program or product, you need to clear it with your boss and the company's communications department. It also should go without saying that you cannot use company letterhead for personal or political use.

With online posts or tweets, you should think twice before you write negative comments about your boss or your employer. While freedom of speech may give you the right to say whatever you wish, freedom of speech will not protect your integrity or highlight your maturity. Instead, those nasty comments that temporarily made you feel so good, might permanently damage your professional reputation.

If you don't like what your company stands for, or you can't stand your boss, take positive action to find a new position. Don't ever consider trying to undermine your employer by exposing confidential information or by relaying trade secrets to others.

Reversing A Bad Decision

We do it all the time—make a decision and then rethink it. Sometimes, we completely reverse it. Most decisions are personal and small. Will you go to your high school reunion? Will you join a gym? Will you spend vacation with your parents? Other decisions, such as buying a house or changing jobs, are bigger and can have a bigger impact.

In the workplace, decisions carry their own consequences. Each day, you probably make many small decisions, most of them so routine that they are barely noticed. Some, however, may have the capacity to enhance or threaten your career progress if they aren't handled correctly.

For example, making decisions about a new hire or terminating an employee are big decisions. Staff turnover is expensive, and insufficient staffing can derail a project. As a result, it's generally useful to have more than one person interview a potential employee. Doing so can provide additional insight to help you with the decision. Likewise, talking with human resources or your own supervisor before deciding on a termination is almost always a good idea.

If the candidate you select for that critical position does not make it through probation, your judgment may be called into question. But, retaining an employee you feel won't succeed in the long run, simply to avoid the embarrassment of having made a mistake, is an even bigger mistake.

As a supervisor, a manager, or even as the boss, you want to make decisions that are evidence-based and well thought out—you want to hedge your bets. Despite the thoroughness of the research, or the recommendations of others, or your own best guess, you will make some bad decisions during your career. How you manage these mistakes is almost always more critical than making them in the first place.

First of all, it's important to admit to the mistake and reverse the decision as soon as possible. Righting a wrong decision is always better than living with a decision that you know is wrong.

If you change your decision, explain your reversal to your boss or your staff. Make your explanation as simple and as complete as you can. Don't blame others. If the final decision was yours, admit that you were wrong.

Next, lay out your plan for correction. Discuss what will happen and when. What will be different? What additional data are needed? What is the timeline for course correction?

Then move forward. Dwelling on past mistakes serves no purpose. What counts is how you convert that mistake into success.

Thought Pioneers

You've all been in the room with a creative thinker. They are the ones known for "thinking outside the box." In a brainstorming session, they can come up with idea after idea. They are often quick and witty, and you may wish you were more like them.

Every organization needs one or two creative thinkers to help other staff think more broadly. Creative thinkers, however, may not be particularly detail-oriented. They may not be planners or implementers. These activities require a "thought pioneer."

The thought pioneer is the person who can envision the path and picture the horizon. She maps and charts the course and finds ways around potential obstacles and detours. She can move off the beaten (corporate) path when needed, and is skilled at knowing what is required and how to manage both for the short run and for the long haul.

If you find yourself in this office explorer role, there are several important skills you should keep honed. First of all are your listening skills. Be open to new ideas and new approaches. Listen carefully to what others have to say and contribute. Listen without immediate judgment and don't be distracted by the background noise of the naysayers.

Next is team leadership. Realize that planning a long trek or a big project requires teamwork, support, and interdependence. As with any expedition, each person on the team has a valuable role to play. They all need to stay focused and fully participatory.

Preparation is critical. Be prepared for surprises, setbacks, and contingencies. Recognize that you and your colleagues may be moving outside of your comfort zones, even charting new territory. Alter your path if necessary, but always keep the vision and your destination in sight.

Most administrators recognize the value of having staff with various skill sets. They know that creative thinking is essential to the development of new ideas and products, but they also realize that the actual journey to implementation takes a thought pioneer. So instead of feeling like you fall short on creativity, give yourself credit for what you and your team contribute on the march to success.

Becoming Professionally Humble

Some people are great self-promoters. Others seem humble, almost self-deprecating. As a professional, and as a leader, how do you find the correct balance?

One way is to practice professional humility. This does not mean having a low opinion of yourself. In fact, it is quite the opposite. Secure people are often the most humble. They don't have to build themselves up at the expense of others. They don't have to be "credit grabbers," always trying to be in the spotlight or appear indispensable.

What it does mean is giving credit. It requires supporting your staff and personally accepting responsibility when things go wrong. It also means being a part of your team and being a trustworthy boss.

We all know the supervisor who starts every report with the pronoun "I." I did this, I completed that, I found the answer or saved the account. You begin to wonder why she or he even needs a staff. These individuals are more interested in self-aggrandizement and personal success than they are helping their staff grow or in highlighting team accomplishments.

Then there is the person who is self-referential. When introducing a speaker or an award recipient, she or he begins with an overview of their own achievements as though they are in direct competition with the person they are introducing. For example, "I first met Ms. Smith when I was giving a talk at ...," or, "Ms. Smith started working for me as an intern, and ...." Oftentimes, they give more information about themselves than about the guest of honor.

There is an appropriate time to talk about yourself and your achievements. When you are asked to do an annual self-evaluation, you do want to note your personal successes. At the same time, it is important for you to recognize growth areas and, perhaps, even failures from which you have gleaned some valuable lessons.

As you become more senior, more experienced, and more secure in your own abilities, you will find it much easier to be generous with your praise and support. At that point you will also recognize that great leadership is not possible without professional humility.

SECTION 5
SO YOU'RE A GROWN-UP NOW

Giving Up Your Helicopter

Everyone knows the definition of "helicopter parent," a term used to describe parents who constantly "hover" over their children, directing their activities, solving their problems, and providing career and life advice. Sometimes, helicopter parents go a bit too far—calling teachers, coaches, college professors, even bosses, when they think their son or daughter has been overlooked or underappreciated, or when there appears to be a problem that they think their child needs help solving.

If you have had an "overcaring" parent like this, you might still be comfortable with your parent helping you make decisions, giving direction, and running interference. You may not have needed, or learned, some of the problem solving skills required to be successful as an adult, especially in the professional workplace.

Perhaps, though, you have been trying for years to get out from under the helicopter. You want to make your own decisions and solve your own problems. How do you get your parent(s) to back off?

If you find yourself with a parent who still wants to be involved in your daily life, ask yourself if you are contributing to the situation without realizing it. For example, do you contact your mom or dad frequently when something goes wrong or when you are uncertain about how to handle a situation or a problem with a colleague or a boss? Maybe you are only looking for sympathy, not advice, but helicopter parents are so used to solving your problems that they can't help themselves.

Second, are you working at becoming financially independent or do you turn to your parents every time there is an unexpected expense? Do you know how to develop, and live, within a budget? Can you focus on essentials, or do you have difficulty delaying gratification and ask your parents to pay for things you can't afford? Are you still using your mom's credit cards? Do you take your laundry home for your mom to do, and does she still purchase the presents for you to give relatives or sign your name on holiday cards? All of these behaviors keep your parents intricately involved in your life.

Finally, can you afford an apartment and living expenses? If you have decided that it's too expensive to live on your own, have you found a roommate or two to split expenses with, or have you decided to move back home to the comfort of your old room and the comfort of your parents' support and intervention? (Note: There can be emergency situations—such as a sudden layoff from your job, or an accident, or serious illness—that leave little choice but to move home for a short period, but you don't want to get stuck there.)

If any of these situations are applicable to you, it may be you, and not your parents, who is perpetuating the helicopter relationship. If that's the case, there are numerous ways to go forward. Begin by limiting the number of texts you send them on a daily basis. Stop asking for advice on minor issues or involving them in your problems at work or with your friends. Also, make a plan and a timeline for ending financial reliance on your parents and stick to it.

Becoming independent is a requisite for becoming a fully functioning adult. No matter how grown up you feel, you can't claim independence if that helicopter is still flying overhead.

Your Office Needs To Grow Up, Too

When you were a teenager, you probably had a bedroom that reflected your teenage interests. Maybe you had movie and concert posters and pictures of your favorite singer and of all your friends. Your college dorm room may not have been too different. Perhaps you switched to travel posters, playbills from shows you had seen, and memorabilia that related to your college or university.

Now you have an office. It might be an eight by ten cubicle or a regular office. There may be two desks, or, if you are lucky, you might have a single office to yourself. Regardless of its size, you would like to personalize it, but want to keep it looking professional. How can you achieve that goal?

First and foremost, a neat, organized office shouts professional. In contrast, if every flat space in your office is covered with papers, file folders, notebooks, and magazines, you appear sloppy. Empty coffee cups and food containers are even worse. Dead plants make you look careless, as do water stains on desks and carpets due to overwatering.

If your company permits the hanging of personal artwork, pictures, and certificates, comply with the request to avoid taping things to a wall or hanging things yourself. Anything taped to a wall looks like your college dorm room.

Before you start to decorate, observe the offices of others. What appeals to you and what doesn't? You are usually better off with a few tasteful pieces than trying to fit in an entire collection. Also, keep in mind that there generally are rules about any pictures or objects that have the potential to cause discomfort among coworkers or clients. In many workplaces, depending on your organization's mission, this includes items of religious significance or anything of a sexual nature. Political items may also be discouraged, particularly if your organization is state or federally funded.

Think carefully about what personal items you choose to display. Each picture or object will invite a conversation with colleagues and visitors. Do you want others to know where you went to school, what you majored in, and when you graduated? If not, hang your diplomas at home. Are you comfortable talking about your partner and children in a business setting? If not, keep their photographs and your wedding pictures at home or on your laptop or phone.

If you have received an award or trophy for being the outstanding employee or the highest grossing salesperson, these may be appropriate items for your office. However, trophies from high school and college or intermural sports simply appear juvenile. You have moved beyond that age-related activity and you can no longer rest on your collegiate laurels.

If your computer screens are visible to visitors, keep the screen savers neutral. A collection of travel photos invites comment and moves you into the personal realm once again.

Your office is an extension of your life and your personality, but more importantly, it's part of your professional brand. Its decor may shout recent college graduate, or a home away from home, or a professional on her way up. Decide what message you are trying to convey and decorate accordingly.

Life Insurance? You've Got To Be Kidding

If your organization offers benefits, life insurance is probably one of them. Frequently, there is a group life insurance program, and you are covered for one or more multiples of your salary, or a certain set amount, while you work there. Many employees pay little attention to this perk.

No one intends to need life insurance at an early age, and it almost seems like bad luck to give it too much thought. If you have no one like a partner or children or parents depending on you and your salary, you might view the availability of life insurance as nice, but unnecessary.

Stop for a minute and think. Who would pay for your funeral and burial if you should suddenly die? The average funeral today costs over $7000. Even cremation has a hefty price tag attached. Would your parents or siblings try to cover these expenses if you were uninsured? If you have a partner or children, is there money in savings that could cover the unexpected costs? If you die, they will have to manage on a reduced income because your paycheck will be missing. Can they also absorb funeral expenses?

The cost of life insurance goes up with every birthday, and if you are diagnosed with a life-limiting illness, life insurance becomes difficult to buy or is prohibitively expensive. That's why a group policy at work is valuable.

So give some thought to the life insurance coverage your employer provides. If you are transitioning to a new position without life insurance, or if you are leaving the workforce for a time to go back to school or to start your own business, check to see if you can convert your employee insurance plan to a term life insurance policy that you buy and maintain yourself. These can be relatively inexpensive, and since the premium is based on your age, you'll never get it at a cheaper price.

While you are thinking about it, check to be sure that the beneficiary you have selected to receive the insurance payment is still current and correct. If a parent has died, or you no longer have the same life partner, or your children have become adults, change the beneficiary accordingly. Your ex-spouse has no obligation to give the money to your current spouse or children if he or she is still named as your beneficiary.

Most of us are uncomfortable thinking about our own death or the death of a loved one, and thinking about life insurance takes us down that path. Yet, having a life insurance policy to help defray immediate expenses or provide income for your family is actually a gift you give them. It should also give you some peace of mind.

Some Conversations Are Harder Than Others

When someone brings up the importance of planning for your care if you become too ill or incapacitated to make your own healthcare decisions, the natural tendency is to try and change the subject and avoid the topic. You may think, "I'm young and healthy, I don't need to do anything about this now."

Every year, healthy young adults are involved in traffic accidents, skiing accidents, and falls while hiking. They are hit by cars, fall down dorm steps, and are injured playing sports. Still others are victims of violence or take an accidental overdose of recreational drugs. They also can contract an infectious disease like meningitis that can become life-threatening.

Your next thought may be, "Well, if I need someone to make decisions for me at a critical time, my parents (or spouse or sibling) will step in." It's not quite that simple or straightforward. You may be engaged, but that doesn't give your fiancé the legal right to determine your care. Or you may be married, and your spouse, not your parents, has the last word. Sometimes the values of two different people or groups are in conflict. For example, your parents may believe that only God can decide what should happen. They will want doctors to do everything possible to keep you—their child— alive. However, you once told your spouse that you would not want to live if you were in an irreversible vegetative state. Without explicit written directions and the selection of a health care agent or proxy (the person you authorize to make decisions for you when you can't make them), you may not have your healthcare wishes honored. You may also inadvertently create conflict between loved ones that can never be repaired.

Most people have never had a conversation about critical or end-of-life care with their loved ones. Do you know what your parents would want if you had to make decisions for them? Do they know what you would want? What about a spouse, partner, or a sibling? Have you ever directly talked about it? Written it down?

As tough as these discussions can be, they will never be any easier than they are today. It is much better to have these conversations while you and the people you love are healthy and able to express your wishes for care, before a crucial decision is looming.

Promise yourself that this is the year you put your healthcare wishes on paper and assign responsibility to an individual for the decisions that would need to be made in a crisis situation. Legal forms (called advance directives) for your state are quite easy to find online. Once you complete, sign, and date an advanced directive, give copies to your loved ones and your doctor. Then encourage your family members to do the same. Someday, you may be quite grateful that this conversation, as difficult as it was, took place when it did.

What You Don't Know About Your 401(K) Might Be Taxing

Most employees lack a good understanding of their 401(k) plans. They know it is a way to save for retirement, but they may not understand its importance, how it works, and why they shouldn't touch it.

A traditional 401(k) plan is a structured savings plan offered by your employer to help you save money for your retirement on a tax deferred basis. They are called 401(k) plans because they are described in section 401(k) of the Internal Revenue Code. There are several different types of plans, and plan rules can vary from employer to employer, so what you have in this job may differ from your last one.

Some employers choose to make regular contributions to each employee's employer-sponsored retirement plan. The amount of the contribution may vary, but it is usually a small percentage of your salary. This is an excellent benefit. You don't have to use part of your own salary to fund your 401(k).

At many workplaces, though, 401(k) plans are self-funded. This means that the amount of money going into your account depends on what you elect to contribute from your salary. This is still an important benefit because the money you contribute is pre-tax, and the interest you earn is tax-free until you retire or withdraw your money.

In addition, many employers encourage employees to save more by making a matching contribution up to a certain percentage of what the employee contributes. This also is a good benefit as it is extra money you are getting each year from your employer. This money is yours once you become vested in the plan.

One problem with 401(k) plans is that employees sometimes treat them as a savings account, and they withdraw some or all of the money before they reach retirement age. This is not the purpose of the benefit, so to prevent this, the IRS has strict rules about how and when you can withdraw funds, and serious tax penalties for early withdrawal.

Once in an employer-sponsored 401(k) plan, you can't close it while you are still employed with the company offering it. You can withdraw your 401(k) savings and close your account when you leave a job. This may be tempting, but it's actually a bad idea. You will face significant tax consequences, and, unless you are 59 1/2 or older, you pay a ten percent early withdrawal penalty.

It's important to learn about, and understand, your specific employer's 401(k) plan. Contribute as much to it as you possibly can. Do your best to take advantage of the employer match if there is one because this is free money. Most of all, try not to borrow from it, or withdraw your money if you change jobs. It is meant to be a long-term investment in your future. It should be untouchable.

Who Benefits From Your Benefits?

Starting a new job is fairly chaotic. You may be trying to transition from an old job or moving to a new geographic location. There are so many details and loose ends to tie up. Sometime, usually during your first week, you meet with human resources to fill out the forms for company benefits. You may have to make decisions about what type of insurance coverage you prefer, including an individual or family policy, an amount of deductible or co-pay you are comfortable with, and whether you include options like dental or vision care. You also may have to think about life insurance and some type of retirement account, most frequently a 401(k) plan.

Several of these forms require you to list a beneficiary, an individual who will receive your accumulated benefit if you die. If you are young and healthy, you may not give this requirement much thought. If you are single, you may list a parent; if married, your spouse. These choices are usual and acceptable. It gets a bit more complicated if your only living parent is ill or if you have other situations like being divorced with young children. You also need to consider how the benefit would be handled if your parent dies, or if you and your spouse died at the same time in a car accident, or some other tragic situation.

Your human resources representative should be able to answer any questions you have. If she is not an expert in benefits, you can contact the insurance or financial company directly to get advice. If you use a financial adviser, you may want to have a discussion to be certain what you decide is in line with your financial and life goals.

After all the forms are signed, most employees never give them another thought. Years may pass, and they never review or update their beneficiaries. This is a mistake. If your life status changes, your beneficiaries may need to change, too. For example, you may have listed your mother as your beneficiary for your life insurance policy. After marriage, you probably want to change it to your spouse. Without formal action, being married won't automatically change your insurance beneficiary. Or perhaps years ago, as a single mother with small children, you had listed your sister as the beneficiary for your 401(k). Your kids are now older, and it is no longer necessary to have your sister overseeing their lives.

It is important to do a beneficiary "check and change" every year or two. It may be helpful to establish a regular time to do so, like on your even birthdays, or on your wedding anniversary. Also, review is required any time there is a major life change, such as marriage, divorce, birth of a child, death in the family, or a new job.

You may also want to encourage your partner or parents to review their own policies on a regular basis and let them know of the changes you make to yours.

Worrying about beneficiaries may be low on your list of life's priorities. There is so much that is more urgent, so much to do just to get through each day. In addition, most people never expect, and almost never plan for, sudden life changes. Having your benefits and beneficiaries current and in order goes a long way if a life crisis occurs.

Don't Co-Sign Your Credit Away

Many individuals underestimate the responsibility and risk they are taking when they agree to co-sign for a purchase, a loan, or a lease. Usually they agree to be co-signers for a relative or close friend whose credit is insufficient to complete the transaction on their own. That means they are lending their credit rating so someone else can secure a loan. This may include student educational loans, loans for the purchase of a condo or car, a rental lease, or a line of credit to start a business.

Too often, the co-signer doesn't know how to say "no" even though they may be uneasy about the situation. Co-signing a legal document for someone else puts their credit, and perhaps even their financial security, at risk.

We have all heard the horror stories and situations: the person who lets her car insurance lapse for a brief period and then totals her car; the roommate who finds major repairs are needed after co-signing for purchasing a condo; a business downsizing or closing shortly after an employee takes a new job and relocates with an iron-clad rental lease; a relationship that ends a few months after co-signing for a small business loan. Financial liability doesn't end because a car is demolished, a home floods, or a job or relationship ends.

The worst case scenario is that the borrower can not make payments as required. The loan then goes into default. This will lead to serious consequences, not only for the person who borrowed the money, but for the person who co-signed the loan or lease. The co-signer may be asked to pay off the loan, may be responsible for late fees, or may be sued by the lender.

At a lesser level, the borrower is making payments, but misses a month now and then, or is frequently late with payments. These are all factors that affect the co-signer's personal credit score, and their credit rating may be damaged without them even realizing it. Or, the terms of the loan may change and the co-signer may not be notified. Also, their credit limits may be constrained by the amount of the loan they agreed to co-sign.

If you are asked to be a co-signer, give it a great deal of thought and get an attorney to review the transaction. It is best to have a formal contract with the individual getting the loan (this is different from the loan contract).

If you are the person asking a relative or friend to be a co-signer on a loan, think carefully about the risk you are asking them to take. Can they afford, and are they willing, to pay off the debt if you can't do so due to a layoff, an unexpected illness, or some other life-changing event? Are you certain you can make the payment and make it on time each month? Since you were unable to secure a loan for yourself in the first place, are you being realistic about the debt? Perhaps it is a better idea to defer the purchase or loan until you can do so without putting anyone's credit—including yours— at risk.

Be A Student Of Student Loans

Going to college or graduate school is often a necessary step toward achieving one's career goals. However, this commitment includes obligations that many students don't fully understand. The average college graduate owes around $30,000 to $40,000 in student loan debt.

This number continues to soar with each graduating class. Further, it's easy to emerge from graduate school with upwards of $100,000 in debt. Add on the interest and fees that accompany these loans, and the debt can become a lifelong obligation that begins as soon as you graduate. Yet, many young professionals underestimate the impact of this responsibility.

Beginning your professional career with tens of thousands of dollars in debt can have serious repercussions, especially if you are entering a field where salary expectations are not particularly high. It may take decades to pay this off. If you are spending any excess income on loan obligations, it means that you won't be saving for a car, a house, a family, or any other personal goals you've set for yourself. It can even impact your relationships as you and your partner take on one another's debt obligations through marriage.

Before taking on significant debt, it's important to fully understand how it will impact your personal and professional goals. First, how much debt will you acquire by earning a specific degree and what are your salary expectations? There are plenty of online calculators which can help you determine how many years it will take to pay down your debt. If the numbers don't add up, perhaps a different degree that offers a wider variety of career opportunities and a higher earning potential would be a better option.

It is also important to consider the university you are attending. Tuition varies dramatically at different schools and it's rarely worthwhile to go into significant debt for the bragging rights of a top-tier, yet expensive, school. The best option is almost always a school that is less expensive or is offering you financial assistance. Most often, a degree is a degree regardless of the institution. You should also explore the career services offered by your university. Do most students find employment immediately upon graduation, or do they tend to run into barriers finding a job?

As you consider different schools, make sure to explore all of your options. Are there resources available that can help you with financial aid such as merit-based scholarships or research assistantships? Schools often have funding set aside to help students pay for their education. If you don't ask about these opportunities, you'll never know what is available. If you are currently employed, you might also have tuition reimbursement benefits. They may not be advertised or discussed often, but if a tuition reimbursement policy is in place, you should inquire about it.

If you've already graduated with significant debt, there may be programs that can help you pay down your loans. For instance, public service may be rewarded through loan forgiveness. It will also be important to set a budget for yourself that incorporates your loan obligations. Paying off loans quickly is important to avoid excess interest and fees.

Education is very important. It is often the key that unlocks career opportunities. However, before you take on significant debt in acquiring your degree, think through the potential consequences and make informed decisions based on your ability to pay for your obligations.

FICO Fitness

Credit scores reflect a person's credit status based on a number of factors. These scores indicate to lenders the risk they are taking by providing individuals with credit (for things like a credit card, home mortgage, auto loan, or business loan). They are used to determine the credit and interest rates lenders may be willing to offer them. Credit scores are used by a variety of vendors and companies to make determinations about whether someone should be granted access to products, services, and opportunities.

There are three main credit bureaus: Experian, TransUnion, and Equifax. They each have their own credit scoring models based on statistical analyses. Even though the different bureaus may use the same measures, your credit scores can differ with each bureau. The most common credit score measure, known as the FICO score, is used by 90% of lenders and ranges from 300 to 850. A higher score indicates to the lender that the individual represents a lower risk. Lenders all use different methods to determine who they will lend to, which means that there is no specific number to aim for, however the higher a score is, the better the chances a person will be approved by a lender. An individual must also have enough credit history in order for a score to be calculated. This includes at least one credit card account that has been open for at least six months or more.

Credit scores change with time, and there are ways to improve them. These include always paying bills on time, keeping credit balances low, eliminating (or not applying for) extraneous credit cards, paying off debt instead of moving it to different cards, and securing against identity theft. Avoiding bankruptcy is another obvious strategy to prevent damaging credit scores. Consumers should also understand the power of good debt—debt from things like car, mortgage, or student loan payments—that have been paid off on an agreed upon schedule. It's also important to know that every time a credit score is checked, there is a slight penalty that lasts for one year on the person's score. This is because the more a person checks a credit score, the more likely it is they need to use additional credit. Improving credit scores does take time, as histories are kept on file for at least seven years, but these tips can help to incrementally change them.

Sometimes potential employers will ask if they can access a credit score. This is most often done to analyze the level of risk and responsibility a job applicant shows. Although they typically cannot access this information without a job applicant's approval, it is something to consider as one more piece of the credit score puzzle.

The Fair Credit Reporting Act sets limitations on how credit scores can be accessed and used. It promotes accuracy, fairness, and privacy of information in the files of consumer reporting agencies. It is important to understand the rights offered by the Fair Credit Reporting Act and use the information if necessary to advocate for yourself.

Predicting The Unexpected

Nearly every young person lives on a tight budget. As a result, choices have to be made, and there never seems to be enough discretionary income to do all that needs done. This sometimes results in being "penny wise, but pound foolish." It can mean putting things off or cutting corners that will result in bigger expenses and more time expended in the future.

For example, your antivirus software needs renewed. You keep putting it off, and then, suddenly, you find your computer has been compromised. Or you put off renewing your driver's license. Then you need to make an unexpected trip for work, and when you get to the airport, you can't clear security because your driver's license is outdated. Or that bathroom leak becomes a flood, or you no longer hear that knock in your car engine because your car won't start. The issues can be endless.

Part of being a responsible adult is planning for emergencies and contingencies. You need to keep track of expiration dates, warranties, and when maintenance or service updates are required. Making a list of important dates and putting them in your calendar can be helpful. When did you last get a new battery or tires for your car? When is your car insurance due? When does your lease expire? Dates like these are critical.

There are other dates and deadlines that are equally important. How often do you update passwords? When is your grandmother's birthday, or when do you need a deposit for that vacation rental? These may seem trivial, but missing them can have a negative impact.

Personal planning is not especially difficult. It just takes a little organization and effort. Financial planning, especially for unexpected expenses, is more challenging. With some foresight, though, you can turn much of the unexpected into the expected and budget accordingly. That approach is cheaper in the long run, and you can be both "penny and pound wise."

SECTION 6
ADAPTING TO LIFE'S CHANGES

Wanting And Having It All May Be Two Different Things

We all have dreams for our lives. Some of them are more realistic than others. When you were little, perhaps you wanted to be a fairy princess and a mommy and an astronaut, all at the same time. As you got older, the combinations might have changed, but, generally, you still saw several interconnected roles in your future. Years ago, though, women didn't have as many choices, and some of those choices used the conjunction "or" rather than "and." You could be a mother or a career woman. You could go to graduate school or get married. You could remain single or have children.

In the ensuing decades, as more choices became possible, the belief was that women would select many roles. They would want to "have it all." Having it all meant they would find a partner, have two or three children, and pursue a professional career, or at least have a paying job. Added to this list might be supporting their partners' careers, volunteering at their child's school or at church or in the community, and helping aging parents. Few women could successfully fulfill all of these obligations, and certainly not at the same time.

Today cultural trends regarding marriage, motherhood, and work are changing. Women are getting married at later ages, and many women are choosing to remain single. In addition, almost three-quarters of women with children under eighteen are in the labor force. Research further shows that the average woman takes only ten weeks off for childbirth before returning to work.

There have been some workplace advances that have helped women manage their multiple roles. The Family Medical Leave Act of 1993 gave employees (both women and men) the right to take 12 weeks of unpaid leave for childbirth or adoption, or to provide care for a seriously ill relative. Some organizations offer flexible work schedules, or the opportunity to work from home. These can be invaluable when trying to merge work and family commitments.

Before accepting a job or moving to a new company, explore options that are, or might become, relevant to your family situation in the future. Be sure you understand employee benefits related to having children. For example, family medical leave, which protects your job while you are out, only applies to employers with 50 or more employees, and you must have worked for your employer at least 12 months. Ask about short term disability insurance which may help provide income when having a baby. Also check whether the health care insurance policy covers children, and, if so, at what cost. These will be important if, and when, you have children.

It is also useful to check for workplace flexibility. Are there personal days available each year? Is it a "family friendly organization?" Can you work from home if your child gets ill? What is their policy on snow days if schools close? If you are interested in furthering your education, check to see if the employer has tuition reimbursement or if you can change your work schedule to accommodate a needed class. Ask about policies related to taking a loan from their 401(k) program if you have a family financial crisis or want to buy a home or send a child to college. Most, if not all, of these topics should be covered in the employee handbook. It's a good idea to ask for a copy before you formally accept a job.

Whether or not you "want it all," you should still prepare for life's changes and challenges. A lack of preparation may limit both your choices and those dreams you have.

Feeling Sandwiched

The term "sandwich generation" was coined many years ago to refer to women who have responsibility for the care of their parents or an elderly relative while they are trying to raise their own children. It's an apt analogy. When fewer women worked, the task of caring for older family members almost always fell to the daughter, frequently to the one who lived the closest. Today, most women hold jobs and they live further from their relatives, making this situation even more complex and difficult.

In addition, many women find themselves trying to juggle multiple responsibilities and commitments in situations that don't involve an elderly relative. This can include dealing with step-children or in-laws, or a sibling who is ill, or a close friend who is down on her luck. These situations can all lead to feelings of stress, perhaps even to resentment.

Self-preservation and balance become important components in sandwich situations. Finding some time for yourself, and learning to say "no" without guilt are two important steps. At first it may seem positive to be needed, but even being needed can wear thin. If you begin to think someone is taking advantage of you, you are probably right. It may be time to set some limits to what you can do or contribute.

One cue that the situation is getting out of control is if you begin to feel indispensable, to feel that only you can do something, or do it right. Feeling indispensable is one of the first signs of burnout.

If you find that caring for one relative or friend is starting to get in the way of your job or other close relationships, you will need to address the situation head-on. If that doesn't seem possible, speaking with a counselor skilled in the area may help you navigate the possible landmines.

Enlisting the assistance of others to offset some of the needed care can go a long way. Buying as much help as you can afford—to help with household chores, for example—can also reduce your overload and alleviate some stress.

It may seem selfish to think about yourself when your step-child has problems, your sister is ill, or your best friend is unemployed, but it is important to do so. Losing your job, getting into a negative financial situation, or becoming ill yourself will only make the sandwich situation worse.

Build A Back-Up Posse

As a professional woman, you recognize the need for back-up plans. You have to know whom you can call and count on when something goes wrong or when you need quick assistance. If you have children, you realize how essential good support is. In fact, you probably have a list of individuals you can rely on (partner, mother, or neighbor) if your child gets sick at school or if there is an unscheduled snow day.

The same plan should be in place for work problems and emergencies. If you're the boss, you more than likely have some staff to do your bidding. If your computer system isn't working, you can call your IT department. If your flight to an important meeting is cancelled, you have an executive assistant to figure out alternative arrangements.

If you're not the boss, you may not always have formal workplace back-up. That makes it important to establish your own support team—a posse of colleagues, friends, and mentors who can, and will, assist you when you need some help. Perhaps you have always been friendly with a guy in another department who is a computer wizard. Or you have a colleague who loves getting deals for airlines and hotels. Or your old college roommate is expert at editing or statistics. And, of course, there are your mentors and friends who serve as a confidential sounding board. These types of connections are invaluable, but they do require some maintenance. Make certain you reciprocate when you can and always acknowledge their assistance. A small gift during the holidays, or flowers, or a bottle of wine when some major favor has been performed, goes a long way.

Your posse needs to include various types of individuals, some of whom you pay for services. For instance, do you know a career coach or counselor you can turn to if you are struggling with a problem that is interfering with work or home life? Do you have ready access to medical professionals if needed? Do you have a pharmacy or drycleaner that will deliver prescriptions or pick up clothes?

To be a professional woman requires both organizational and delegation skills. To weave together your professional career and family responsibilities requires even more effort.

Many high achieving career women suggest that you hire as much help as you can. That is good advice, but it is just as important to cultivate a personal and professional support system of people you know and trust.

Disclosing A Health Issue At Work

Our health is intensely personal, and most people like to keep medical issues private. Sometimes, however, it is almost impossible to keep a health condition or illness quiet, especially if it requires you to be absent from the office for several weeks or months. Your colleagues will note your absence, and will be naturally curious. You will need to decide what information you want disclosed to your workplace and to your colleagues.

There are several important laws related to illness and work. Some address privacy and your right to have your health information protected. Others, like the Family and Medical Leave Act (FMLA), protect your job when you are sick.

FMLA provides for 12 weeks of unpaid leave in a 12 month period when you are seriously ill. It also requires that your employer maintain your same health benefits while you are on FMLA, but you do have to continue to pay the same portion of your health care premium while you are out. Also, your employer is entitled to require you to use any vacation, sick, or personal time while on FMLA. (You would, of course, receive pay for these days which might help financially.)

There are some restrictions for this law. Your organization has to employ 50 or more staff within a 75 mile radius, and you must have worked there for at least one year, and worked at least 1250 hours in the previous 12 months. If you are requesting leave through FMLA, you will have to have a medical certificate completed that states that you can't work due to a serious medical condition, but you do not have to disclose a specific diagnosis. If this is your preference, be certain to tell the physician completing the medical certificate and your health care team that you wish to keep your diagnosis private.

Other important factors about FMLA are that the leave may be used intermittently (for weekly treatments, for example), and it can be used to request a shorter work week if required by your medical condition. Your employer also must make reasonable accommodations to enable your return to work.

While you generally can't be required to tell anyone about your illness (a worker's compensation claim would be one exception), sometimes it's not possible, or plausible, to try and keep an illness completely private. For example, you might become ill at work, or you may have to have a surgical procedure that has some residual effect like needing to walk with a cane. Some treatments, like chemotherapy, also can cause noticeable side effects such as hair loss.

While there are examples of workplace discrimination due to a medical condition, for the most part, employers are understanding and supportive. Also important is for your employer to know whether any special precautions are needed after your return to work, or what might be required if you have a medical emergency while there.

In addition, workplace secrets are difficult to keep, and trying to do so may add to your stress. Instead, think about how you can handle disclosing only what you wish to disclose. When colleagues ask questions, the best course is to simply say something like, " I had to have knee surgery," or, "I was diagnosed with cancer, but I am doing fine now." If they persist with questions, you may need to cut off further discussion by saying you really don't want to talk about it, that you just want to move forward and get back to normal as best you can. Then, do just that.

Private Change Or Public Conversation

When you get new glasses or change your hair color or style, a few of your work colleagues may notice and remark on it. Usually the only response you need is to thank them for their compliments. When you are working on changing your weight or fitness level, however, the conversations may be harder to manage. You don't want to be discussing your weight loss techniques at a staff meeting or in front of your boss.

People rarely realize how insensitive they sound when they make comments like, "You've lost a ton of weight. What are you doing?" Or, "You look great. You must feel a lot better." Or, "You look ten years younger." They may think they are complimenting you, but they are back-handed compliments at best. Again, your response should just be a simple "thank you," as you quickly change the subject to a more appropriate topic.

Perhaps you find the positive comments encouraging, and you feel like your colleagues are cheering you on. Even if this is the case, it still puts you in a strange position with the focus on diet or fitness outcome rather than work product.

Make certain you aren't unconsciously calling attention to your change efforts (and yourself). You can graciously decline lunch with colleagues without adding that you can't go because you're afraid you'll go off your diet. Don't make your gym activities the topic of water cooler conversation. If you need to work late, don't grumble about missing your yoga session. If someone brings in donuts or other snacks for the group, don't berate them for tempting you.

It is almost always best to keep your personal life private. Conversations about your health, your weight, or your physical fitness (or lack of fitness) usually don't have a place in the work setting. They often are as awkward for others as they are for you. So keep the focus on your professional accomplishments, not on your personal challenges, successful or not.

Don't Postpone Positive Action

When you enter the professional workforce, constantly moving forward is hard work. There is so much to juggle that it is easy to feel overwhelmed. Sometimes the desire to simply coast for a week, or month, or year seems attractive, almost seductive. What happens when we find ourselves unmotivated or bogged down in our personal or work lives?

Many factors can be roadblocks to success. For example, health issues can sap energy. That cold you can't kick, that recurrent neck pain, or frequent stomach problems could be the result of your body reacting to increased stress. A physical exam will help you rule out a serious condition and might be all you need to get back on track.

Disappointments are another barrier. You may be feeling discouraged because a promotion or raise didn't come through, or you can't seem to get ahead financially. Or, perhaps an important relationship has changed.

You find yourself feeling like you want to withdraw from the world you've worked so hard to create.

Tough times signal the need for re-evaluation. They also may require careful planning and putting some new strategies in place. What doesn't work when things are difficult is burying your head in the sand, sabotaging yourself, engaging in self-destructive behavior, or acting out.

Instead, you need to take positive action. If your problem is physically-based, adhere to the health care plan prescribed for you, or maintain your exercise regimen, or get more sleep.

If your roadblock is emotionally based, talk to a mental health counselor, or supportive friend. Feeling depressed and sad is exhausting. It can also cloud your judgment and make you overly sensitive. Check to see if your company provides an employee assistance counselor who offers confidential services.

If you have a work-related problem that you can't seem to resolve, contacting a trusted colleague or mentor could help you devise a plan for correction. Or perhaps your human resources department could assist with the situation.

If you are having financial issues, seek some expert advice to help you establish a budget or savings plan or to manage credit card debt. There may be ways to consolidate your debt or expenses that will alleviate some of your stress.

The worst thing you can do when faced with a serious life or work obstacle is to do nothing. Problems in one area of your life can, and do, spill over into other areas and negatively compound the original situation. The longer you postpone taking charge of the situation, the harder it becomes to resolve it.

You've spent years getting ready to climb that career ladder. Don't let inaction knock you back down.

Preparing To Be A Stay-At-Work Mom

When you are planning to start a family, it is important to think through how you will balance work demands and navigate potential career challenges. As you read the following information remember to stay flexible. Babies are notorious for bringing joy as well as interrupting the best-laid plans.

Before you get pregnant, check your healthcare benefits. What does your policy look like in terms of maternity coverage? Have you found a doctor yet and are they covered by your plan? You will also need to determine if your doctor delivers at a specific hospital, and if so, is that hospital in-network for your plan?

Next, you need to review your benefits. No employer is required to provide paid family leave. The Family and Medical Leave Act (FMLA) only requires your employer to hold your job for you for 12 weeks, unpaid. It also only applies to individuals who have been employed for over one year in an organization that employs over 50 people. Employers not covered by FMLA may still choose to provide maternity benefits, so make sure you fully understand what is available to you.

Based on your benefits package, you should determine when you plan to begin and end your maternity leave. Factor in if your company offers paid maternity leave, and if so, for how long? You may want to use your vacation and sick days (however some of these might be needed for the many medical appointments you will attend before you give birth). You might also qualify for short-term disability benefits, but you need to determine what percentage of your salary will be paid to you and for how long. Although you are going to be excited about becoming a mother, it's critical to first outline your budget and forecast the amount of time that you can actually afford to take off. You should also consider how much money you need to have saved before your baby arrives.

Once you've outlined your personal plan of action for maternity leave, you will need to determine when you will tell your employer. You should check to see if there is a company policy regarding disclosure. FMLA requires women to disclose their pregnancy 30 days before anticipated leave. It is wise to alert your employer of your intended absence so that the organization can take action in case they need to temporarily fill your position or ask colleagues to fill in for you. You may also wish to take a proactive stance and outline a plan as you both transition out of the workplace and back into your position.

Many women do not disclose their choice to have a baby until after the first trimester and before physical changes make it evident. Some women choose to tell their boss first, particularly if they have a close relationship. It may also make sense to first tell your human resource department. If you are supervising staff, you may want to tell them immediately after you disclose the news to your boss or human resource department and it's wise to tell them all at the same time, and offer some details, particularly regarding your expected timeline and whom they will report to in your absence.

It may be challenging for a pregnant woman to be fired, it can and does happen. Although the Pregnancy Discrimination Act forbids prejudicial treatment of pregnant women, it does not mean that you cannot be fired for unrelated reasons. The Americans with Disabilities Act also requires employers to make reasonable accommodations for pregnant women. However, this only applies until the situation "would cause significant difficulty or expense." The Fair Labor Standards Act and Affordable Care Act require employers to provide nursing mothers with adequate break time and a private environment to pump breast milk for a year following the birth of her child. It's also important for you to understand state laws and how they can impact your employment. If you feel like you are being discriminated against, keep a record of what was said and done.

It's important to think about your boundaries once your baby has arrived. Decide if you are willing to be contacted regarding work, and if so, who can contact you and how would you like them to touch base? Be specific, but flexible, as your schedule might change once the baby arrives. If you are open to contact, tell colleagues to expect a text or return email within 24 hours.

As you prepare your transition back into work, will you be arriving earlier than usual and leaving at 5pm sharp? Will you be more open to emails after your baby is sleeping? Do you need to guard your time during work hours, making long coffee breaks a thing of the past? Be clear about your priorities, and protect and promote what is important to you.

The more you can prepare as you plan your pregnancy, birth, and maternity leave, the better your transition in and out of work can be. Use cautious optimism as you plan and be flexible with yourself, your partner, your baby, and your career.

Note: If you are planning to adopt, much of this information will apply to you, but make sure that you verify the specifics.

Stepping Back In

Many women step out of the workforce for a period, and there are varied explanations for a career pause. Possible reasons include a relocation due to marriage or a partner's job transfer; a layoff or being terminated; a return to school for an advanced degree; an opportunity to live or travel abroad; a pregnancy or adoption; or to care for an ill family member.

Regardless of the reason for the absence, re-entering the professional workforce will take some advance planning. First of all, you will need to check on the status of your field. Has much changed since you were out? What are the current developments and issues? Have you kept your license and certifications up to date, and, if not, what do you need to do to regain your credentials?

If you had a previous mentor, contact her and ask for an update or any leads she can suggest. If you are still close colleagues, you might consider asking her to be a reference. If possible and feasible, you also need to track down one or two past supervisors as potential references.

You will also need to update your résumé. Take time to explore changes in current résumé construction and electronic job listings and applications. Depending on the length of time you have been out of the workforce, the format for job applications may have changed significantly. If you need assistance, check continuing education classes at your local community college, or various women's conferences, or professional groups.

Sometimes the hardest part of returning to work is deciding how to explain your absence, especially how much personal information you want to disclose. It's generally best to be forthright and non-apologetic.

Simply stating that you took several years off to raise your children, or a year to care for an ill relative should suffice. Finishing a graduate degree or getting married are other fairly easy explanations.

It gets a bit more challenging if you were terminated. You never want to falsify records or be untruthful. You also don't want to be defensive, or blame your previous boss, or say negative things about your old employer. It's a good idea to practice what you are going to say. If you have a colleague who works in human resources, or a friend who has done some professional hiring, ask them to help you think of possible interviewer questions and answers for them. It also might be useful for you to role play the exchange.

If you find you are overwhelmed by the prospect and process of returning to work, think about contacting a career coach or a placement agency. While these have a price tag attached to their services, it can be an important investment in your future.

Strategic Job Hopping

There is a widespread belief that millennials are job hoppers. Compared to their predecessors, perhaps this is true, but it may not necessarily be a bad thing. Switching jobs may be an essential step in achieving career goals. Leaving a position may be in pursuit of a better title, higher salary, and/or expanded duties. No one should feel trapped in a job that is no longer serving their best career interests, but it is also important to recognize a balance before taking that next step.

Strategic job hopping can be positive. Many people view their first position as a starter job. Fresh out of college, employees often need to learn basic skills such as how to navigate the workplace, create and maintain professional relationships, adhere to timelines, write for a professional setting, create budgets, communicate appropriately, and network. Unless there is a clear ladder for career progression, once that initial skill set is acquired, it may be time to think about a position that offers new opportunities and experiences.

Oftentimes an ideal job is not one you seek but rather one that is offered when you least expect it. Exceptional performance is noticed by others and may be rewarded through competing job offers. Weighing the pros and cons of staying versus leaving is a personal process. Some people value stability so staying at a predictable job can be very assuring. Others might aspire to climb the career ladder quickly and see switching jobs as the best way to realize their goals.

There is also the issue of positions that just aren't the right fit. Both hiring managers and potential employees take a chance with one another. That leap of faith, however, does not always work out for the best. No job is perfect, and it's important to try to figure out how to succeed even with barriers in the way. At the same time, life is too short to be miserable in a job that just isn't a good fit. If this is the case, it may be time to look for a new position. However, if this is repeatedly the case, it's time to reevaluate your career. Are you actually in the right field? Do you have consistent challenges interacting with colleagues? Is an office job the best setting for you, or should you be your own boss? What do you need in order to be successful? An honest, comprehensive self-evaluation can be a vital tool to figure out the best career path.

As you navigate your career, it is important to remember that a résumé full of short-term positions can be a red flag. Employers take a risk by hiring someone new. They invest not only money and time in a new hire, but also trust that their commitment to a new employee will be mutual. If an organization is worried that a new employee will quit after only a year or two, it may not be worth welcoming them aboard.

A career is a marathon, not a sprint. It can be helpful to have a map in mind which sets a path for your professional pursuits. Just don't be surprised if you reach a fork in the road and have to make decisions you didn't anticipate. Think about both the bigger picture—the story you tell with your career decisions and where your path will ultimately lead—as well as the details of daily life—the happiness and significance you derive from your work. This balance can be challenging, but it will help you craft a career that is valuable to both you and to others.

Too Good To Be True

The 2014 Employee Viewpoint Survey conducted by the government's Office of Personnel Management found that millennials who accept a position with a government agency stay slightly less than four years.

If you are in your 20s or early 30s, four years might seem like a long time to you. You may fear getting locked into a job or missing new opportunities. You may have been told that the only way to get ahead is by changing jobs so that you continue to grow both your salary and your expertise.

On the negative side, employers may be reluctant to hire workers who job hop. They figure they invest time and money in the recruitment and training process, and if an employee leaves after a short period they have not realized a return on their investment.

When a new job opportunity appears on your horizon and it looks too good to pass up, make sure you do a full assessment. Remember the job you hold now also looked good when you secured it.

There are several things to consider before you make a jump. First, salary is important, but will your benefits package and flexibility be the same or better?

You may receive a higher salary, but find the extra dollars are quickly offset by the portion of the cost of benefits, like health and dental insurance, that you must pay. Similarly, you may assume your leave time is equivalent, then find you are can't take vacation during a probationary period which could last six months or more.

The vesting period for benefits like life insurance and 401(k) plans begins again and may be longer than that at your current place of employment. Also, if you go to a smaller organization (less than 50 employees), FMLA (family medical leave) may not be available.

Next, workplace culture and flexibility in the new job may not be as suited to your personality and needs as your current job. The new workplace may be comfortably multigenerational, or persons in your own age range could be few and far between. This means you may be surprised by either the casualness or the formality of the organizational dress code.

There may be more stringent policy guidelines regarding flex time, personal time, or using workplace computers. There may be less (or more) administrative back-up for routine things like copying documents or preparing meeting materials or doing routine follow-up. Perhaps most importantly, you may find that you don't have an actual office, but have a work cubicle instead, which can cut down on both productivity and privacy.

Another consideration is that access to your boss and other organizational leaders may be different. Those employees or team you really liked during your interview may work in a different area or department, and you may have little contact. You will need to adjust to a new managerial work style. Perhaps your current boss has an open door policy, and you can easily drop in with a question or suggestion. The new boss may limit interaction and see staff by appointment only. Or vice versa. You function best in a collaborative environment, but the new one is much more hierarchical. Or you like the predictability of a set reporting structure and are less comfortable with group responsibility.

Last, but not least, will the new organization really value what you bring? You may figure that if they hire you, they must recognize your skills and potential, but will they also value your creativity and innovation and your desire to make a difference? Will you be able to start work at the top of your current skill and expertise level, or will you be relegated to the beginning professional role again?

Will you be able to jump right in or will there be a long (and slow) ease-in period? Will you have to sit on the sidelines while you wait for orientation and a probationary period to end? You may find that the new organization's software systems and methods of operation are outdated. Will you feel that it is a waste of your time and talent to go backward, or can you be an asset in moving the organization forward?

We know that younger professionals may be able to adapt more readily to different workplace cultures, different management styles, and organizational policies than many workers who have been around and entrenched for years. On the individual level, however, you need to understand your own capacity for flexibility and adaptability. What do you value most in a workplace? What are the trade-offs for you? How important are benefits versus salary? In what type of work culture are you most likely to be successful? How important are diversity, personal growth, and breadth of experience?

The new position you are thinking about may be just right for you and may be an important move forward in your career. Or, it can be a disappointment, and you will find that the job you left had more opportunity and security.

Job hopping can be positive or negative. Be certain you look before you leap.

SECTION 7
PROFESSIONAL DO-OVER

Making A Dull Job Shine Again

When you first began your job, there was an excitement. You had things to learn and things to try. There were new colleagues, new ideas, and endless possibilities. You were at the starting point with no end in sight.

After four or five years, that perfect job may have lost some of its shine. The routine may be comfortable, the problems predictable. You know the annual schedule of work events like the back of your hand. You also have come to know many of your colleagues along with their quirks. The sameness can sometimes overwhelm you. You feel as dull as the job.

What would it take to bring back the shine, to make the work day sparkle once again? You can start by making some changes at the personal level. Do you have flexibility in your schedule? Can you change your routine—start and end the day earlier? Is there a nearby gym you can join? Can you take a walk at lunch instead of eating at your desk? Can you work from home a day or two a week? These small changes can make a big difference in your outlook, but how can you change the job itself?

Start by doing a workplace assessment. Are there new projects starting? Can you get assigned to lead one? Are there internal or external continuing educational programs of interest for which your employer will cover the cost? Are there any new job openings expected in the next few months for which you would be eligible?

Don't let your restlessness interfere with your performance. Set up a time to talk with your boss. Do not tell your boss that you are bored. Instead, tell her you are looking for a challenge or two to add to your experience base. Perhaps it is time to try supervision or to participate more fully in the departmental budgeting process. If relevant, tell your boss that you would like to be considered for a higher level job when one becomes available, that you feel you are ready to move forward professionally. She may or may not agree that it is the right timing for advancement, but at least you will have planted the seed that you are ready to try new things and are looking for opportunity within the organization.

Changing employers is not always a step forward and there are many reasons to stay employed in the same organization for a specified period of time. You may not yet be vested in the pension or 401(k) programs. Your job may have excellent benefits that you need and that you can't match elsewhere. Your commute may be short, and your work hours flexible. You may be eligible for a bonus or pay bump at the end of the year. Your partner or best friends may work nearby and you carpool to work. Perhaps most importantly, this was a job you wanted. It's what you planned to do in your career, and it's a good fit for you.

If you have reasons for staying, find a way to polish that job rather than junking it.

Don't Compound A Career Challenge

Sometime in your career you may come to a barrier that seems insurmountable. Perhaps you lack the credentials for promotion to the next level. Or you scored poorly on the test for the position you wanted. Or you got fired because you didn't reach a goal, or because you screwed up somehow. Or a coworker got the job or promotion you were expecting. These can be formidable obstacles, but most career obstacles can be overcome. The following are some tips for meeting the challenge head on.

Don't compound the challenge. When angry or upset, people sometimes make hasty—even disastrous—decisions. Don't quit and walk out because a colleague got the promotion you were expecting. Don't accuse the human resources manager of favoritism, or unfairness, or discriminatory practices. Don't insult your boss. Don't say negative things about your organization, and stay away from social media rants. In short, avoid bridge burning at all costs.

Do a thorough and honest evaluation of the situation. Include a close friend or two or your spouse or partner in your review. Did anyone really think your organization could, or would, waive the requirement for a law degree or CPA credential for that next job level? Is there a pattern of only men getting promoted and you are being discriminated against because you are a woman, or did two women just get promoted last year? Don't seek blind support (even though that might feel good), but get some factual input. Were you being naïve and too hopeful, or should you have been selected? Were you actually the person responsible for missing that goal, or are you a convenient scapegoat?

Once your emotions are under control and you are ready to have a professional conversation, set up an appointment to talk with your mentor or a trusted colleague at work. Ask for their perspective and for suggestions for moving beyond the current situation. You can express disappointment, but don't make excuses or try to place blame on others.

If you find yourself at a crossroads, consider hiring a career coach. If you repeatedly seem to run into the same barrier time after time, you might find such a coach useful. Are you unrealistic about your capabilities, or do you need practice in selling yourself? A career coach can help you sort out the issues and help you make any needed adjustments.

If you decide you really want to move in a certain direction, you may have to get further education or training, or acquire a requisite credential. If so, explore possibilities. Does your current employer offer tuition assistance or pay for credentialing expenses? How can you prepare for the next step in your career?

Finally, realize that almost everyone faces career challenges at some point in her or his career. Comparing yourself and your level of success with others serves little purpose. It may simply make you feel anxious, or depressed, or resentful. However, much can be learned by observing how others successfully overcome career set-backs.

A job may span a few years, but a career goes on for decades. What seems to be a stumbling block today might actually be the starting point for your next big opportunity. Try your best to keep your current challenge in perspective and keep moving forward in a positive way.

Refresh Your Résumé

It's easy to forget about your résumé, especially if you've been in a position for some time. You might think that you only need to update your résumé when you are applying for a new job, but it's important to keep it current on an ongoing basis.

It can be a challenge to remember all of the work you've accomplished. If you keep a running list of your responsibilities, projects, and achievements, it will be easy to plug the most relevant ones into your résumé. If you need a curriculum vitae (CV), it is even more vital to keep it updated. A CV includes all of your presentations, publications, and career-related accomplishments. It can be particularly challenging to keep this up to date unless you do it on a regular basis.

You never know when you will need your résumé. Even if you have no plans to apply for a new job, perhaps your current company will hire a new CEO who will want insight into all employees. If you are applying for a promotion, it may be company policy to request a new version of your résumé. Don't put yourself in a position where you will have to scramble to create a document from scratch.

You should also create a version of your résumé for online platforms like LinkedIn. Many employment opportunities come from social media, and your profile should reflect your current career path. If you've recently gained new skills or taken on new responsibilities, make sure that your profile reflects that. Many people even have personal blogs or websites that include their résumé or CV as well as writing samples, accomplishments, and accolades for their work. Such an online presence can be an impressive first impression for future employers.

Résumé formats also change. It's common for résumés to incorporate graphic designs or illustrate skills visually. This can take time to create so it's important to research and practice with online software programs (many of which are free) to create a compelling résumé.

Although it requires a bit of planning and time, it's much easier to continually refresh your résumé than to rush to update it only when you are looking for a new job.

Time For A Mentoring Makeover

If you've been working for five, ten, or more years, you probably have someone you turn to as a mentor. Maybe it's a trusted colleague, or a former boss, or someone you met from another organization who has been interested in you and your career. Mentors are invaluable. They offer objective feedback, good advice, and unconditional support.

There may come a point, however, when you find you have outgrown your mentor. You may have moved to a higher position on the organization chart than your mentor occupies. You might have changed direction, and your mentor doesn't have the technical or area expertise to assist you in your new role. Perhaps your mentor has retired and no longer stays active or in touch with your professional field.

All of these are good reasons to seek a new mentor. You also might feel that you are doing quite well in your career and do not need as much mentoring, or you need mentoring of a different type. Or perhaps it is time for an executive career coach.

If you are fortunate, you will have a series of individuals willing to serve as a mentor at specific times in your career. Be certain you choose them wisely. They should always be supportive, and, while the mentoring relationship may be a mutually supportive one, it should always be focused on your best interests. If it becomes competitive or negative, it should be ended.

So what do you do about the mentors you have outgrown? Stay in touch with them, but on a less regular basis. Keep them informed about promotions and career milestones. Every chance you get, thank them for their part in your career success. An old saying seems relevant with regard to mentors: make new friends, but keep the old, one is silver, the other gold.

Update Your Personal Brand

Your attitude. Your message. Your abilities. Your actions. Your words. Your appearance. Your essence. All of these things make up your personal brand. You broadcast it each and every day, in the office, online, and in every interaction you have. Your brand is even comprised of what you choose not to do such as declining invitations to networking events or happy hours.

Your personal brand is entirely within your control, and it can, and should, evolve and grow with your career. If you are a leader, you have to be calculating with your brand. This means that you put serious thought into the different components that others use to perceive you. If you don't care what others think, you are putting yourself at a deficit and robbing yourself of potential to achieve your goals.

If you have your sights set on being a leader in a particular field, health for example, your brand should reflect that. You should stay on top of health news and communicate to the world that you care about these issues. That might mean populating your social media accounts with related articles you find interesting or attending functions where healthcare thought leaders congregate.

If you want to be taken seriously, but your personality leans towards silly, your analysis of your brand should take that into consideration. You might be the life of the party, but you may not be considered a credible professional. At the opposite end of the spectrum, if you are always extremely serious and people don't feel comfortable around you, that can be a barrier to collegiality.

Your reliability is also a big part of your brand. Do you follow through on your promises? Do you meet deadlines? Do you show up to meetings on time? No one wants "flaky" included in their brand description.

A more superficial brand concern is appearance. Unfortunately, it's a shortcut for others to judge you. Consider your profession, field of practice, and workplace. Do people wear suits every day? Are jeans necessary to fit in? Are your hair and makeup choices distracting to others? It may not be enjoyable to consider these things, but it's necessary to create a strong brand that communicates your personality in a positive way.

If you aren't sure what your brand looks like, ask a trusted colleague or friend who knows you well. Request the top three words they would use to describe you. Demand honesty. If those words are not characteristics you want to be associated with, it's time for a personal brand overhaul.

Shop Your Closet

If you've been in the workforce for a while, chances are that you have acquired a decent wardrobe. It may be tempting to keep up with trends and constantly shop for new clothes, but that can be a drain on your wallet. Most professional women have clothing options that they don't always use effectively.

You probably have a few wardrobe staples that you consistently rely on—for many of us that means black pants or skirts, button down shirts, or a go-to suit. However, if you take the time to go through your wardrobe, you can donate the clothes that you no longer wear and rearrange your closet so that you are inspired to put on pieces that haven't seen the light of day in a while.

It can also be helpful to browse websites like Polyvore, Pinterest, and Instagram to get outfit ideas. Many times you have the various pieces you need to create new looks, but you haven't thought about how different items might be paired together. Simply search for "work or career outfits" and recreate the looks or put your own spin on them.

Accessories are also important to help keep your look fresh. A statement necklace can completely change an outfit. Don't go overboard though—both in terms of cost and how many accessories you wear to work at once.

When you do shop for work clothes, it is always wise to invest in classic pieces. If you consistently purchase trendy clothing, you will probably find that it goes out of style by the next season. Classic doesn't have to mean boring, but it does help to create a professional look that lasts.

The money you save from shopping your closet can add up quickly and can be invested in your 401(k), used to purchase something you need like a new computer, or saved for something fun like a vacation.

Finding Your Career Center

One of the popular questions for children is, "What do you want to be when you grow up?" When a teenager gets to high school, the question changes only slightly to, "What are you going to major in when you go to college?" Neither question is particularly useful because the young child and the teenager both lack enough life experience to make an informed choice.

Eventually college students sort through the hundreds of possibilities and find one that seems relevant and exciting to them. If they are lucky, they will choose one that will serve them well throughout their career. It will become their career center.

College, though, is not an endpoint. It's a springboard to the next level, to finding that first professional job. That first job isn't an endpoint either. It's only the first rung on a tall career ladder. In fact, it is estimated that the average person will change jobs ten times during her or his working life.

Careers can take many different shapes. They can be linear in design, with an individual moving from one job to another similar one, just with enhanced responsibility and perks. Or a career may follow a more circular route. For example, if a woman gets a college degree in English, she may begin working as an editor, and then decide to move into speech writing for an elected official. Or she may begin by teaching high school English and decide later that what she wants to do is become an online blogger or book author.

What happens if what you have centered your career on is no longer what you love or are interested in? If you feel you are on the wrong career path, begin planning today for how you can change course. Will a career correction require you to get additional training or education? Will you need to relocate? What impact will changing careers have on you and your family?

On the other hand, if you know the field you have chosen is the right one, yet you are not content with what you are doing, you may simply be in the wrong job. That's a much easier correction than changing careers completely.

To have a successful and rewarding career, you need work you like, work that you are good at, and work that is meaningful to you. If any one of these elements is missing, it's important to do a thorough review to find out why. Then you need to determine how you can get back on that career path that you were looking for when you began your professional journey. You may have ten chances to get it right before you retire, but, in the end, ten unfulfilling jobs isn't really much of a career.

How To Avoid Presentation Arrogance

Most professionals have had a course in public speaking or communication 101. If you took these courses, you know all about doing the prep work, using media selectively, and arriving early for your presentation. You have been coached in avoiding "ah" or "like" as filler, and not using jokes unless they are culturally and situationally relevant and you are good at telling jokes (which few people are).

What you may not have been taught is what many seasoned audience members consider presentation arrogance. The following four examples can be particularly irritating.

The first is the presenter who begins with, "Good morning," and then waits for the audience's response. If it isn't robust, the presenter raises her voice and says, "Let's try that again—good morning!" This tactic is understandable if you are a motivational speaker whose role is to get the audience warmed up, but it has no place in most presentations.

This is similar to the after lunch speaker who stops midway and asks the audience to stand and stretch to keep them awake. If your presentation is interesting enough, they won't need to participate in your forced activity.

The last two are used during periods of audience discussion and question and answer sessions. Repeating the same phrase after each comment can be a distraction and can seem arrogant, like a presenter who says, "Thank you for that question," after each question, or saying "absolutely" every time someone speaks. It can sound obnoxious or condescending. Eventually, people will focus on the overuse of the words or sayings and no longer listen to the actual answers.

The last example is one that seems to be used everywhere at the moment. An audience member asks a question, and the presenter responds with, "That's a good question." That response shouts arrogance. It's like saying, "I'm surprised you are smart enough to ask an intelligent question." In many instances, it's used to give the presenter a moment to formulate an answer, but she would be better off by simply taking a quiet moment before she speaks.

As you advance through your career, make note of what works and doesn't work in professional presentations that others make. Then select what might work to help you become a more proficient speaker, and avoid the arrogant pitfalls along the way.

Danger! Opportunity Ahead

Sometimes it feels like others get all the breaks. They always seem to be at the right place at the right time. Your best friend was lucky to stumble across that great new job. Your sister had that summer internship that turned into a paying position. Your colleague had dinner with some senior staff from his organization and is now working on an exciting project. Why don't these kinds of things happen to you?

The lucky breaks above probably didn't just happen. Opportunity is seldom as random as people make it sound. An intern might spend months trying to impress her supervisor and secure a permanent position. Perhaps weeks of background work went into securing a role on that special project.

In order to have "lucky breaks," you must be open to opportunity. You also need self-confidence and be willing to trust your instincts. For example, would you have jumped at that great new job your friend accepted, or would you have been more cautious? Are you always on the lookout for challenging projects, or do you feel you already are overloaded and can't take on more work right now?

The downside of opportunity is risk. Sometimes taking advantage of an opportunity does require quick decision making, and that can be risky. Most often, though, you have some time to think about and consider the pros and cons of an opportunity. The main point is not to let fear or your cautious nature close off opportunity too quickly and completely.

A second point is to prepare for opportunities. Keep your résumé up to date, and your passport current. Save a few vacation or personal days to have time available in case someone requests an interview, or asks you to attend an exploratory meeting, or a great business travel opportunity presents itself.

Finally, try to evaluate your own tolerance for risk. It might be helpful to ask your family and friends how they view your risk-taking behavior. If you are especially risk adverse, you probably won't be able to take advantage of many new opportunities, unless you believe they are a fairly safe thing. On the other hand, you also don't want to be risk-reckless and put your financial security or personal safety at risk.

If your tolerance for risk is low, try increasing your risk capacity little by little. Begin with smaller risks—introducing yourself to a keynote speaker, asking for a meeting with a possible mentor, taking a trip without every detail being planned, or even simply trying new things. It's difficult to move outside of your comfort zone, but being more open to risk also makes you more open to opportunity.

Own It

Entrepreneurs are different from most of us. They are innovative risk-takers who prefer to start their own business rather than work for someone else's organization. This may have been their ultimate goal as they obtained their education, or they may have arrived at the decision after working for someone else for a few years. Perhaps their family operated a business, and they were part of that endeavor while growing up. If so, they understand the dedication and time it takes to open and run a business.

Starting a business, no matter how small, is hard work. It is not simply an escape from the tedium of the daily grind, or the desire to escape a bad manager, or a way to set your own schedule. It requires vision, capital, perseverance, and the ability to take an idea from conception to execution. It also requires a strong business skill set that includes planning, management, fiscal oversight, leadership, marketing, and team building.

Regardless of potential risk, you may have a strong belief in your idea and you are confident you have the ability to make a start-up successful. Before you quit your day job, take the time to do the necessary research, to build your capital, and plan for your personal needs. Start-ups generally don't offer benefits like health insurance or annual bonuses. Many times they don't even provide a salary for the first year or so.

Be certain your plans are as realistic as possible and free from "wishful thinking." This includes your launch timeline, marketing requirements, and, especially, potential revenue generation. Be prepared for expenses to outpace revenue for the first few months. Also, try to keep some money in reserve for business emergencies, such as technology issues or market turndowns.

You may be considering securing a small business loan. This can be an excellent solution as long as you don't put other parts of your family life, such as your home, at risk. To obtain a loan you will need more than a good idea. You will also need a solid business plan and a good sales pitch.

Finally, be prepared for some setbacks, maybe even for some failure. Most great entrepreneurs have experienced failure after failure, but they didn't let it stop them. Instead they took what they had learned and applied that knowledge to future endeavors.

Success in small business may not be a straight line, and you may frequently have to resort to course corrections. However, if being an entrepreneur is your dream, you need to own it.

We all know the image of the starving artist or author who sacrifices everything to practice their craft. This is not the same as being an entrepreneur. While artists can grow a following, they seldom grow a business. Both undertakings take creativity, but the skills brought to the task differ.

SECTION 8
SELF-IMPROVEMENT NEVER ENDS

Inner Strength Inventory

Inner strengths are similar to talents. The difference is we may not fully recognize or acknowledge our inner strengths, so they remain hidden, even from ourselves. Understanding and owning your inner strengths can be an asset to your self-confidence and to your job performance.

As an exercise, ask your closest friends or family members if they could describe one or two strengths that they think you possess. You might be surprised at what is mentioned, terms like self-discipline, optimism, perseverance, kindness, a disarming sense of humor, enthusiasm, or fairness.

You might also hear some descriptors that could be perceived as positive or negative. Examples are words such as competitive, perfectionistic, or carefree.

Negative words might also come to friends' minds. Do they perceive you as being stubborn, divisive, disorganized, or driven? Do they think you care too much, work too hard, or allow yourself to be swayed too easily?

Once you have gotten some feedback, assess what you have heard. Does it match how you perceive and describe yourself and your strengths? What surprised you? What are the areas where you disagree with family or friends?

For example, you are competitive, but you work in a competitive environment. You wouldn't last long without your competitive spirit. Maybe you are driven, but you love the challenge and you love what you do. You can't wait to get to work each morning. Or you realize that perfectionism can be positive or negative, but in your line of work, detail is imperative.

Be as honest in your assessment of yourself as you can be, and make a list of the identified strengths with which you agree. Then think about strengths you think you have that no one mentioned. These are your hidden strengths.

Perhaps you have a "never say die" attitude. You simply don't quit when something becomes a bigger challenge than expected. Or you know you have great stamina and can keep at a task until the job is done. Maybe, when needed, you have a laser focus and can determine what's essential about a project and what can be jettisoned. Or you can be an excellent listener and can help the team clarify a problem or an issue. If fairness is one of your strengths, you might be the conscience of your team, and you may be the person who is counted on to provide a balanced view.

You might also take a look at your last performance evaluation and listen carefully when you are being evaluated this year. Your boss's assessment can offer further insight and clarification. Are you described as a "go-getter," a team player, a hard worker, a good thinker, or a dedicated employee? If so, add these strengths to your growing list.

The more you recognize your inner strengths and what you can and do bring to the workplace, the more self-confident you will feel. Knowing that you have personal resources that you can draw upon when needed lets you be more resilient and helps you to overcome setbacks and disappointments. Your inner strengths may be hidden from others, but they should never be hidden from yourself.

You Drive A Hard Bargain

Each of us occupies numerous roles such as spouse or partner, mother, daughter, sister, and employee. You may also be a community volunteer or a member of a local club or sports team. These roles compete with one another for your time and attention.

Unless you are a person with few personal responsibilities, you will find yourself engaging in frequent role bargaining. If you are a parent or the caregiver for your own parents or an elderly relative, you may have to deal with role bargaining on a regular, even daily, basis.

Role bargaining can include bargaining with other people for time and support, but, most often, role bargaining is intrapersonal. You bargain with yourself.

For example, the mandatory budget meeting is scheduled for Wednesday afternoon, the very day that your son's little league season opens. Or it turns out your organization's annual conference or trade show is scheduled the same weekend as your niece's wedding. Or the only doctor appointment your mother could get coincides with the monthly staff meeting, and your boss hates it if anyone misses a staff meeting.

No matter how organized you are about your calendar or how well you manage your time, conflicts, unexpected events, and emergencies do occur. Good back-up plans, quick thinking, and creativity are essential. Can your spouse attend the little league game and videotape it for you to watch with your son later that evening? Can your sister or cousin take your mother to the doctor appointment? Can you be at the conference for the first two days and take a red-eye flight which arrives in time for your niece's wedding ceremony?

Finding alternatives is actually the easier part. What's harder is beating yourself up because you can't be at an event, or you miss a family celebration, or you disappoint a child, or upset a family member or your boss.

If you listen intently to your self-talk you will hear yourself bargaining with yourself. The bargains go something like this: "If Susie can take Mom to the doctor's this time, I'll drop by and spend Sunday afternoon with Mom." Or, "If John can get to the opening ballgame, I'll try not to miss any more this month."

You might also hear your admonishing self chirping in. This self is the one that lectures you all the time. "You should have been there." "You know Mom isn't comfortable at the doctor's office. She would have preferred you take her instead of Susie." "Yes, you got to the wedding ceremony, but you were the only family member absent from the rehearsal dinner."

These statements are demoralizing. They serve no useful purpose except to punish you for doing the best you can. The next time you find yourself in this situation, try disarming the admonishing self by reframing and restating the outcome. For example, when you hear yourself say, "I should have been there," change the statement to, "I would have liked to have been there." Instead of saying, "I know Mom was disappointed," give yourself some credit. Pointedly say to yourself, "I do the best I can to be an attentive daughter. Mom knows how tough it is for me to juggle my schedule."

It is hard enough to manage all of your various obligations and responsibilities. Don't make it harder yet by second guessing and berating yourself.

Self-Advocacy Is A Required Skill

Sometimes when women stand up for themselves, they are labeled aggressive, or self-centered, even bitchy. As a result, women may be more reluctant than men to take issue with a decision in the workplace that is unfair or that affects them personally. They may want to be seen as a team player or perhaps they are a bit intimidated by an existing old boys' network and are trying to stay under the radar. Or perhaps they simply are unsure about how and when to speak up.

This isn't a problem exclusive to young women just beginning their careers. Many women with years of work experience still struggle with standing up for themselves, their rights, and their ideas.

Self-advocacy requires a specific skill set. Like other skills, these can be taught, learned, and used successfully.

For example, if you feel your opinions aren't heard or are discounted at work, you can learn to be more effective. In a group setting when a discussion ensues, speak up early. It's hard to enter the conversation if you remain silent too long. Watch how others, especially men, interact around a controversial topic or put their ideas forward. Many will compete for floor time, and they can be quite direct, easily dismissing or challenging the ideas or statements of their colleagues. Better yet, watch how a woman you admire handles workplace interactions and how she manages to get her opinions heard and included. Does she adopt the same methods as the men? Does she make very thoughtful and cogent arguments? Does she use humor? If you know her well, ask how she became so comfortable with heated discussions, conflict, and confrontation.

While you will need to develop your own style, observing the way colleagues interact can give you an understanding of the methods and boundaries acceptable in your workplace.

If an issue involves disrespect or unfairness in the way you are treated, the situation may best be handled in a private discussion with your colleague or boss. You should confront the problem as soon after the event as you can, but not before you have a chance to get your thoughts together and your emotions under control.

There are some general guidelines for addressing a difficult work situation that requires self-advocacy. First, choose your timing, and think through your argument or concern in advance. Decide what you want or what you want resolved. Plan your opening statement. Don't start with an apology like, "I'm sorry to bother you," or "I hate to bring this up." Also, ask directly for a resolution or speak directly to the issue. Control your emotion and tone (no tears, no swearing, no raised voice).

If an issue with a coworker can't be resolved by talking it through, or if negative or disrespectful behavior continues, you may need to have a supervisor intervene. If that doesn't work, you may need to speak with someone from human resources.

If the problem is with your boss, it can be much more difficult to resolve. Asking advice from a more experienced and trusted colleague or speaking with a mentor might help you devise a plan or approach.

You may be fortunate and work for a company that has good leadership and that values respect, inclusion, and teamwork. Many workplaces, however, lack one or more of these attributes, and self-advocacy becomes critical. Being willing to stand up for yourself is always a good idea, but in the workplace it needs to be done in a professional way that doesn't make you appear overly aggressive or whiny. With a bit of practice, you can find an approach that works well for you and let's you become your own best advocate.

Competitive Edge

Competition can be a good thing, as long as it's healthy. We have all engaged in some sort of competitive activity at some point in our lives whether it was athletics, academics, or a variety of other situations where our drive to be the best kicks in. Competition gives us a reason to strive to do better and provides a standard by which to measure our own performance. Some of us may be more prone to competitive behavior and find it thrilling, while others shy away from such tense situations. However, by the time we're professionals, and especially a decade or two into our careers, the only person we should really be competing with is ourselves.

Competition and comparison can set the foundation for unhappiness because there will always be someone smarter, better, and faster than we are. This is true for absolutely everyone because we can't possibly be perfect at everything. Setting goals for yourself grounded in your own circumstances and strengths, and based on your personal career vision is the best method for happiness and ultimately success.

It becomes a bit more difficult when others are competing with you. It becomes exceedingly challenging when that person is your boss. If you've shown competence, leadership, and potential, your boss may see you as a threat. It may seem innocent at first—not showing much enthusiasm for your work or even disregarding you, or being overly critical. It might also escalate to preventing you from speaking to other "higher ups," isolating you, or even taking credit for your work. Many times this behavior is, in fact, workplace bullying, but smart bosses will do it insidiously and in a way that can't be easily witnessed by others or traced back to them.

Overt and irrational competitive behavior in the workplace is indicative of low self-esteem and fear. People who are confident and comfortable in their position, and with their skill set and ability don't attack others. In fact, great bosses make efforts to highlight the strengths and accomplishments of their staff members. They shine the spotlight on them and provide opportunities to help them grow. It's important to remember that so you can rise above pettiness and jealousy. Easier said than done, but competing with your boss is a losing game. When you see yourself as the only worthy competition, it can help to keep things in perspective and take off some of the (competitive) edge.

Be Your Own Cheerleader

You know the type of day—you get up and have no energy. You can't find anything you want to wear or anything that you think looks good on you. Your hair doesn't cooperate and by 8:30 you know you are going to have a bad day. And thinking that, you probably will. Our personal attitude and the self-talk we engage in are powerful forces, so powerful, in fact, that they can shape your outlook, your behavior, and your performance in and outside of the office.

We all keep up a running conversation with ourselves. In fact, unless you are interacting with another person or really concentrating on a movie or project, you are engaging in self-talk. Sometimes it's useful to stop and listen to what you are saying to yourself. Are you a harsh critic or an encourager? Do you speak kindly to yourself, giving yourself the benefit of the doubt, or do you play the blame game and beat yourself up emotionally?

When it comes to trying something new, does that inner voice become a coach or a detractor? Do you find yourself limiting new opportunities for fear of failure or because you tell yourself it's too risky? Do you stick to the status quo because it silences that inner voice?

Most children grow up with adults urging them to "be careful." Whether riding a bike, playing sports, or learning to drive, you were encouraged to "take care." And, as adult women, you do need to think about personal safety. Whether jogging after dark, meeting someone online, or traveling alone to another country, you need to consider and plan for factors that present serious risk.

But when it comes to trying something new like accepting that big assignment, training for a half marathon, applying for that new job, or driving in a different country, be sure your inner critic isn't determining your choices or your chances for success. Many times, we fail at something, not because we can't do it, but because we quit too soon. We give up because we convince ourselves that we can't win, that we can't achieve at that level, or that we will fail in the end.

When that inner voice starts sending you negative or constraining messages, recognize them for what they are. They are the remnants of childhood admonitions, of previous times when you didn't try hard enough, or when you tried but still didn't reach a goal. Try to remember that all of those are in the past. This is a new day, a fresh start, and a different opportunity. When your inner voice becomes too loud, too negative, or too limiting, recognize what is happening and consciously stop it and take control of your thoughts. If you do, you will turn that inner critic into the coach or cheerleader that you need.

Your Invisibility Cloak

Not all employees enjoy the limelight. Some are introverted. Some just want to focus on the work at hand. They may be cordial, but they limit their social interaction at the office. They are often thoughtful, only speaking up in meetings when they actually have something important or helpful to say, not just to be a part of the background chatter.

Then there are employees who start off on a fast path but eventually fade into the background. They do an adequate job, often much more than adequate, but they seem more like a fixture than a player.

If you find yourself in category two, it's important to find out how and why you became almost invisible and then plan how you can get back on track.

Perhaps you had a life situation that took much of your energy for a time. Or perhaps you began to burn out and you felt like you needed some time to recoup. Maybe you felt you couldn't compete with the newer hires, that your skills had become outdated. Or, you had a miserable boss and withdrawing became your way to survive. Maybe you just became too comfortable with the status quo. Whatever the cause, it's time for a positive change.

If you find yourself in this situation, start by doing an assessment of current opportunities at your workplace. Is there a new project that you can volunteer to lead? Can you offer to supervise the new intern or help with new employee orientation? If you have a decent relationship with your boss, have a forthright conversation and tell her that you are feeling a bit stuck. Ask for suggestions for moving forward. Or make an appointment with human resources to discuss new organizational possibilities. Set up some networking time with colleagues. Take a hard look at your résumé and see what new skills you need to add to help you get current. Set realistic goals and timelines.

A career spans about 40 years. During that time, there will be high and low points, and a collection of good, mediocre, and poor jobs. You may change profession, location, or direction. There will be many choices along the way. So throw off your invisibility cloak and jump back into the career picture.

When You Think You're The Smartest Person In The Room

Most of the time, we encourage women to speak up, to be part of the conversation, and to take their rightful place at the corporate table. But this chapter is written for those of you who constantly waved your hand in school, certain that you knew the best answer. It's for those of you who have little self-doubt, who always want to be the leader or to be in charge. There is nothing wrong with these characteristics, unless they are actually getting in your way at work.

Ask yourself some questions. Do you ever feel impatient to be heard or to get your ideas across? Do you sometimes talk over a colleague in your haste to provide "a better answer?" During a meeting, do you find yourself speaking more than your colleagues? Does your input sound more like dissent than discussion? Do you volunteer for every assignment or quickly offer to lead the team or project?

If you answered "yes" to several of these questions, it's time to step back and do a bit of self-analysis and course correction. The following are some suggestions for toning down your over-the-top behavior.

Work at limiting and timing your comments at meetings. You do want to speak early and you do want to be part of the conversation, but try to speak only when you actually have something new or important to add. Don't monopolize the conversation.

Do not compete for the spotlight. Let others contribute without debate. Don't belittle a colleague's idea or be dismissive. If it is a poor suggestion, others should recognize it, too. Let one of them shoot down the bad idea for a change.

Don't try to sneak your opinion into the conversation by playing the devil's advocate. Everyone can see through that ploy, and most people hate when others do that.

Wait before you volunteer for an assignment. Your colleagues have probably discovered that you are always willing to do the heavy lifting, and they wait for you to step up. Think about how full your plate already is. Decide if this is a project that you are really interested in. Could it be important to your career? Could you be a part of the project team without being the team leader?

Ask a close colleague to observe your meeting behavior and offer suggestions to help you be more collegial, more of a team player, and less of a take-charge personality. If you have been overly assertive and labeled a "know-it-all" by your peers, an honest discussion can be invaluable for helping you modify your behavior.

This is not to suggest you play dumb or hide your light under a bushel. If you are smart, self-confident, and have leadership capacity, you will go far. Those are great traits—exactly what you need to get ahead in your career. But very smart people can also appear arrogant, smug, impatient, domineering, and condescending—negative traits that work against them and interfere with good teamwork.

You may actually be the smartest person in the room. Just be sure you are using those smarts for the benefit of your career.

Self-Worth Sabotage

Twelve years of grade school. Four years of college. Perhaps two years of a master's program and even untold years pursuing a doctorate or other higher degree. Add credentials, certificates, continuing education hours, reading for enrichment, and networking events galore, and the effort and energy you've put into your career is countless. All of this hard work, dedication, and focus should translate into opportunities for success. It can also set you up for self-worth sabotage.

If your career stalls, or you are unhappy at some point along the way (which happens to most people), it's easy to turn that frustration inward and blame yourself. Perhaps you got passed over for a promotion, felt unheard or unvalued, or you've been laid off, or even fired. Maybe you're simply bored and ready for the next challenge in your life, but that new opportunity simply isn't available quite yet. Anger, shame, guilt, sadness, and a host of other negative emotions are rational when we are faced with career bumps and bruises.

The danger lies in tying your entire self-worth to your career. When your happiness hinges on what happens (or doesn't happen) in the office each day, it's a recipe for disaster. It is perfectly fine to be proud of your work and put immense amounts of effort and energy into the activities on which you spend the majority of your waking hours. However, when work gets you up in the morning and keeps you up at night, causes you to avoid focusing on other areas of your life, and creates extreme amounts of stress, it might be time to reevaluate your priorities and find a way to integrate more balance into your life.

Discipline Your Calendar

Calendar discipline is tough. Depending on your employment level, much of your daily work schedule may be determined by your boss and the demands of your job, but you usually have some choice. For example, many organizations have core working hours with flexible start and ending times. These can be used to your advantage when it comes to managing your workload.

Regardless of your start time, try to actually begin your work day as soon as you get to work. You can greet colleagues and get a cup of coffee without getting caught up in the morning chit chat in the kitchen or hall. If you spend 30 minutes a morning catching up with office gossip and talking with colleagues, in a week's time you will lose over two hours of productivity that you may have to compensate for by working later or taking work home.

Meetings are huge time eaters mainly because few people run efficient meetings. In many organizations, there is a routine structure for meetings, and most committee meetings are scheduled for an hour. We know that work will expand to fill the time allotted, so instead of scheduling a meeting for 60 minutes, suggest scheduling it for 45 minutes, or even 30 minutes. If you are hosting the meeting, start and end it on time.

If you are in an organization where meetings rarely start on time, be on time yourself, but take some work with you. It's surprising how many reports or emails you can get done in the five or ten minutes you spend waiting for colleagues to arrive for a meeting.

If you need to interact with a colleague who has trouble ending your conversations, suggest meeting in his office or in a conference room. It's much easier leaving someone else's office than it is to politely get someone to leave yours.

If you have external meetings, be sure to build travel time into your schedule. Nothing is more nerve-wracking than sitting in a meeting that your boss is running and knowing that you are going to be late for a client meeting. If at all possible, schedule external meetings early so that you can get the meeting out of the way before you go to the office.

Many meetings are now done by conference calls, and few of them are done well. If you are in charge of the call, be certain everyone has the correct call-in information. Send out a reminder the day of the call. Be sure your own system is working and ready. As with other meetings, start and end on time. If it's a call with a chatty colleague, schedule something directly following the call so you have a valid reason to stop the call at the agreed upon time.

It's a useful habit to take a few minutes before you leave for the day to organize your desk and to check your calendar. Review what you have scheduled for the next day and be sure you have necessary items on hand so you are prepared, especially for your first meeting or two.

If you are lucky enough to have an assistant to help you with scheduling, be sure you are clear about what you prefer (for example, amount of time allotted for meetings, amount of travel time required for external meetings, some protected time during the day to return phone calls and check emails).

Finally, keep in mind that you might not have to accept every meeting invitation you receive. Can you send a document or summary report instead? Could one of the team members attend on behalf of the team? Could you attend only part of the meeting that is relevant to you or only attend the first half of a conference call?

As you become more experienced in the workplace, you should also become more expert at managing your calendar.

Setting Bold Decade Goals

Most of us set goals for our lives. Too often, though, we don't think big enough. We may set a time frame for finishing a degree, or buying a house, or making a six-figure (or more) salary. These are all worthy goals, but do they describe what you really want to achieve in your career?

Perhaps it's time to set some super goals—overarching goals that will give you career direction for years to come. If you're in your twenties, choose a major goal for each coming decade. What is your super goal for your 30s, for your 40s, 50s and 60s? Your goals should build on one another and should show a clear path of progress.

For example, if you want to be the CEO of an international business by age 40, what should your goal for age 30 be? One young woman, interested in international work, decided to match her travel experiences to her age. By working for a tour company, she was able to visit 30 different countries by age 30, thus gaining a broad international perspective.

Subgoals for this woman could be achieving fluency in one or more languages, living abroad for several months or longer, finding an international work experience, or finishing an MBA in international business or a law degree in international affairs. Once your super goal for a decade is set, the subgoals become clearer and achievable.

Other examples of decade goals might be becoming a successful writer, achieving tenure in an academic position, becoming an executive director of a national association, or holding an elected leadership position.

Keep in mind that during your career, you will have a limited number of decade goals. Choose them carefully, but boldly, and every year make a list of what you must accomplish to move closer to your next decade goals.

SECTION 9
BUSINESS BEHAVIOR

Value-Based Work

Most of us start out believing we can change the world. We have lofty ideals and dreams for the future. You may have been brought up in a family or community where young people were expected to give back. This spirit may have been intensified by volunteer work in high school or college, and, you thought about starting your career in the nonprofit human services sector.

Perhaps some advisers or relatives discouraged you by telling you that you would never make a decent living in "charity work," or that you would burn out, or that you wouldn't be safe, or that you would be exposed to an unsavory side of life.

Maybe others asked you why you would "waste" your degree in accounting, or marketing, or communications, or business administration by going the nonprofit route. If you wanted to do people work, why didn't you choose a different area of study?

So, you got a job in the corporate sector. The perks are great, but you feel that the focus is only on the bottom line. Profit, not principle, seems to be the driving force, and you find you are uncomfortable with their marketing approach or the way business is done. Selling products or business services lacks civic appeal for you.

Maybe there is a mismatch between your values and the values of your workplace, but don't assume all for-profit corporations are the same. Many are civic minded. One of the best known is Toms Shoes which donates a pair of shoes for a needy person for every pair sold. Other companies donate a percent of revenue or profits to good causes. Many corporations and small businesses are sponsors of community and charity events. In fact, without these contributions, most nonprofits would cease to function.

If you are fairly happy with your job, but still feel something is lacking, donate some of your time and expertise to a cause that is meaningful to you. Volunteers are always in great demand. You can help build a house for a homeless family, or participate in one of the many sporting events held as fundraisers. Better yet, help deliver meals to individuals who can't get out or visit some of the residents in a nursing home, or spend an afternoon teaching computer skills at the local boys or girls club.

If you are still thinking the nonprofit route might be a better values fit for you, explore existing opportunities more thoroughly. Talk to colleagues from that sector, visit some community agencies and foundations, and see how your skills and values fit that business model. No matter where you work, it's never too late to make a difference.

The Go-Along Kid

How often each day do you take the easy way out? You know what a family member or colleague or boss thinks or wants or believes, so you agree or go along with something when it's not the direction you prefer. In fact, it may not even be in your best interest. Think about the following scenarios and whether they sound familiar.

A friend asks you for a favor that not only will inconvenience you, but will cost you time and money, and will create havoc with your budget.

A coworker asks you to cover for her absence or for an error at work. It makes you uncomfortable to do so, but you hate to see her get in trouble.

You really can't afford to be a member of the wedding party for your old college roommate, but you don't know how to decline without hurting her feelings.

You had your heart set on that camping trip with friends this summer, but your parents are expecting you to spend your vacation at the lake with them.

You have been offered the job you hoped to land. You are so grateful you are being hired that you don't want to ask for a higher starting salary. You accept what is offered even though you know it's less than you are worth.

The examples could go on and on. Often, it is simply easier to take the path of least resistance. You go along to get along. Sometimes that is the wise choice—why have that same argument with your sister or partner when the outcome won't differ or it doesn't really matter that much? Why challenge your boss on the same issue time and again when you know she won't change her mind?

However, there are times when that path of least resistance leads you down the wrong path. For example, lying to cover up a coworker's error is never acceptable. Your integrity is important. So is the trust that your boss places in you, not to mention you could be reprimanded, even fired, for lying.

Spending or lending money you don't have because you don't want to hurt someone's feelings is simply foolish. Long after the event is over, you will still be trying to manage your debt and you will find yourself feeling resentful and remorseful.

Agreeing to something you don't want to do also can lead to resentment, or at least to a bad mood. Your colleague asks you to give her a ride home because her car is in the garage. You are happy to help her out today. Then she finds out her car needs a part that will take a week or ten days to get in. Giving her a ride every day turns into a major imposition, rather than a favor.

We all know someone who constantly allows herself to be taken advantage of time after time. You don't want to become that person. If you are that person, it's time for a change.

Learning how to say "no" is an important part of growing up. It may take some practice, but you can become efficient at it. Eventually, you'll be able to say "no" without even adding an explanation or an apology. A simple, "No, thanks," goes a long way when you are asked to join the group for lunch, or attend an event, or contribute to a cause you don't wish to support.

Negotiation is another important skill for the workplace and for our personal lives. It is a skill that can be learned and enhanced. Negotiating compensation when seeking a new job or salary increase takes some practice and perhaps some courage. We have all heard the slogan that "you don't get what you deserve; you get what you negotiate."

If negotiation is important in your job, take a short course on how to do it better.

Negotiating with family can be equally difficult. Telling your parents that you won't be at the lake this summer because you are going camping with friends may be offset by assuring them that you will be home for a few days over the Christmas holidays. Again, the more you use your negotiating skills, the more skillful you will become.

Compromise is another tool, and it can be a bit of an art. The goal is that there is some equality in the result. You get "x," she gets "y." If compromise is always one-sided, you again begin to feel resentful and used. There are, of course, things, like your ideals and your ethics, on which you should never compromise, but there are many small daily decisions where compromise is useful. Just be certain you aren't always on the "giving side." Also, be clear why you are compromising. If it's simply to avoid conflict or to please others, you may need to rethink your stance.

That path of least resistance you take day after day may actually be a long and winding road to nowhere. When you find yourself meandering almost thoughtlessly down that go-along/get-along path, stop for a moment and decide if that is really the direction you want to be going. If it's not, start looking for a different path.

Mentoring Is A Two-Way Street

You know mentors are useful, and you know you should have one. You have thought about contacting an experienced colleague you admire and asking if she might be able to give you some career advice or help you network with a certain group. You're not usually shy about asking for what you need, but you can't help wondering why a successful woman would be interested in helping you.

Let's put aside the fact that many women like to mentor others. Or they may recall how important mentoring was for them when they were climbing the career ladder and feel they should give back.

What you may be underestimating is what you will bring to the exchange. The following things are some examples of what you may contribute to the mentoring process.

Young professionals are a direct link to a new generation of women. Every generation has its own characteristics, ideals, communication patterns, and difficulties. These are important factors for women responsible for multigenerational workforces. Your mentor can use you as a confidential sounding board as needed, and you might even be able to suggest some changes to office policy or solutions to those thorny conflicts that seem to spring up when each new generation enters the workforce.

In a similar manner, you can help your mentor acquire a broader understanding of current pop culture. CEOs and other executives often exist in a fairly rarefied environment. Unless they live with teenagers or young adults, it is easy to lose context or misunderstand popular trends. They may have a large marketing department working for them, but the final decisions for direction are still theirs. You may be able to suggest additional resources that would be useful in their decision making or discuss a relevant issue or book or movie over lunch or a drink.

Younger people are early adapters. This is especially true with electronics. It may be hard to believe that some people in your mentor's circle grew up with typewriters and mainframe computers. When they were your age, they didn't have access to smart phones or the worldwide web. They still may prefer face-to-face meetings and paper lists to Skype and the Cloud. If asked, you can recommend and demonstrate new technology such as your phone or laptop. If the mentor-mentee relationship is comfortable enough, you may find yourself mentoring your mentor in these particular areas.

One of the most important things you bring to the mentoring relationship is a different viewpoint. While you are there to learn from someone with a wealth of experience and contacts, you don't want to underestimate what you already know. Experienced mentors have made it a habit of learning from others, and they will be interested in what you can teach them. For example, have some theories been changed or dismissed since they were in graduate school. Are new methodologies now being applied. They didn't get where they are by always doing things the same way, and they are often hungry for new ideas.

The final thing you bring to the mentoring relationship is your attitude. This should highlight both the energy and enthusiasm you have for your field and your career. Time with your mentor should be productive and respectful. It is not meant to be a gripe session or a one-sided pick-me-up. While together, learn everything you can and let your mentor know how you have made changes or applied what you have learned. This provides a mentoring feedback loop of sorts and lets your mentor know that her time with you is well spent.

You don't come to the mentoring relationship empty-handed. As you get to know your mentor better, and as you feel more comfortable with the process, you will realize that mentoring is a two-way street.

Don't Be A Digital Dinosaur

Change is perhaps the only constant in the workplace. Whether you are changing jobs, welcoming new colleagues, or taking on new responsibilities, evolution is what propels us forward. Whether we like it or not, we have to embrace it.

One area where this is particularly true is in the technology space. Email keeps us connected. Social media keeps us informed. Databases keep us organized. Apps keep us on the cutting edge. Whether you are 20 or 60 years old, it is vital to stay aware of new technology and maintain a working knowledge of the programs, software, and products that are necessary to do your job.

When you are in a leadership role, it is particularly important that you use technology to your advantage. Staff will count on you for timely responses to emails at the very least. This means that you will most likely carry a smart phone with you most of the time. If your organization utilizes a particular database to track donors or members, you should understand the capabilities of the program so that you know what data are available to analyze. When a decision is made about a budgeting program, you better understand it well lest you run the risk of making uniformed decisions.

Additionally, it is important to understand new technologies even if you don't use them in your daily life. For instance, you may not want to broadcast your thoughts on Twitter or Facebook, but your organization will need a social media strategy to communicate your brand. It also benefits you to understand LinkedIn, not only when it comes time to look for a new job, but to broadcast your personal brand and keep connected to colleagues around the world.

It may seem like there are new platforms launching every day (and there are) which makes it a challenge to stay up to date. However, it is worth the time to be curious about new technologies. You do not have to be an expert, but you do need to seek out these tools and ask questions about them. They can help you engage volunteers, raise money, spread your message, and, ultimately, achieve your goals. You only hurt yourself by refusing to evolve with these changes.

Cast A Wide Net

You've read all the advice about networking. You know it can be important, perhaps even essential, for getting ahead in your field. Each year you promise yourself you will do better, but work and life always seem to interfere. You just don't seem to have time for networking. How do others do it?

If you have a colleague who is very good at networking, set a time to talk with her. Ask her if she has a system, or how she keeps track of individuals she meets. See if she uses a special computer app, or how she determines whom she wants to meet, and if she sets targets or goals for the year.

Planning so carefully may seem calculating and off putting, but networking is a serious activity. It's not a simple random process, even though you may unexpectedly meet individuals who will become close colleagues or collaborators.

Think about creative ways to network with others. Can you use email more effectively? Can you send a note to the author of that article you found so intriguing? Do you use LinkedIn or Twitter? All of these activities can be done without leaving your office. What's important is to set aside, and protect, a certain amount of time each week to keep up with your contacts.

For face-to-face meetings, find a way to keep them brief. Can you meet for coffee before you go to the office in the morning, or can you have a brief chat over lunch at an offsite meeting, or spend fifteen minutes catching up before heading back to the office. This type of networking will not disrupt your work day very much. If you attend conferences, review the program agenda before you go and make a list of a few presenters you want to meet. Be systematic about it.

When pressed for time, it is easy to resort to tunnel vision, trying to network only with the people you believe have the most influence or who interest you most. For networking to be effective, however, you need to cast a wider net. Are there others at your level of expertise who might be good contacts? What about that new hire in the next department who is considered an "up-and-comer?"

Also, it can be useful to move outside your usual circle. A good contact or two from technology, a talented graphic designer, or an expert in human resources might prove invaluable at some point.

Openness to new people and new ideas may be the most important qualities for a good networker. If you exhibit these qualities, you will find that you won't have to do all of the work. Others will be asking to network with you.

Spinning Time Into Gold At Work

If your work schedule requires a meeting every hour on the hour, skip this section. But if you are like most people, you find yourself with some dead periods of 10, or 15, or 30 minutes between meetings or commitments. If you have two or three of these a day, it is like "found" time, almost as good as gold.

You can spend this gold in a variety of ways—chatting with coworkers, balancing your bank account, or taking a brief walk. All of these may be good choices, but they are also valuable chunks of time that can help you get your actual work done. They can help you leave work at quitting time, and they can prevent you from having to take work home with you.

The key to successfully using these little blocks of time is to keep a list of things that require only 15 to 30 minutes to complete, and then keep that list and the work close by. For example, do you need to review that power point presentation for the graphic designer? Do you need to respond to a request for a meeting? What about a writing project? Can it be broken down into chunks so you can write the draft introduction or ending in a 15 to 30 minute period?

Accomplishing things in small amounts of time is mainly a function of mindset (and a bit of discipline). If you think you will need to spend hours on the report introduction, it will probably take you hours. Work will expand to fill the time allotted. But work will also shrink to fit the time allotted. Suppose you simply start writing that report introduction.

Writing experts claim you should be able to write two paragraphs, or around 100 words, in ten minutes. Yes, you will need to edit it later, but editing is so much easier than starting from scratch. Most of our writing evolves. We rarely sit down at our computers with ideas fully formed. Besides, if you write something down, all day long you may be thinking about what you wrote. During your next short period of free time, you may be able to add to what you wrote or change it for the better.

Breaks during the day are important, but so is family time. Or, if you use two free 30 minute periods, you might be able to squeeze in an hour at the gym. The possibilities are great.

It doesn't take an efficiency expert to recognize time wasted. And it doesn't take a genius to know time is money. More importantly, time saved is time you get to spend later. It really is like gold.

Working From Home Might Not Be A Panacea

Working from home is the dream of many employees. It sounds so great—no commute, no having to worry about wardrobe, no petty office squabbles. You can sleep later, do household chores at odd moments, and save on gas, lunches, and perhaps even child care. Who wouldn't find that desirable?

What most people underestimate is how difficult it is to be structured and self-disciplined when working from home. It can be hard to start the work day at a regular time, and it is easy to let the work day expand into the late afternoon and evening hours. Maintaining focus on work can be a challenge when there are so many competing domestic chores or when a child is vying for your attention.

Another problem is presenting a professional image when on Skype or conference calls. Disturbances like a dog barking, a grass mower running outside, the doorbell ringing, or a child crying all detract from the image you are trying to project. People who are working from offices rather than home find these domestic interruptions particularly annoying.

Another concern is whether you have the type and quality of equipment and computer service needed to work from home. Some companies provide laptops or routers. They may or may not pay for Wi-Fi and other useful items like a good conference phone. Again, nothing seems more distracting than to have people fall off calls or being unable to download or send files in a timely fashion.

Working from home also has limitations for assistance from coworkers when needed. Tech support is no longer right down the hall if your email stops working. It may be harder and more time consuming to contact that colleague who is an expert on spreadsheets or the friend who is usually so helpful with editing suggestions for your reports.

For some individuals, one unexpected downside of working from home is a lack of face-to-face interaction. Many people miss the camaraderie of the office, the personal exchanges with friends, and the feeling of being a part of a team or group. There also is the chance that you won't be included in some meetings, especially those that are spur-of-the-moment, or the informal meetings that take place after the planned meeting you participated in by conference call.

The ideal may be working from home several days a week, but going into the office for important meetings and to maintain visibility with your boss and upper management. The old saying, "out of sight, out of mind," can have consequences when a new team is being formed or a new project is being assigned. You also can lose out on networking opportunities with people who could be instrumental in your future career.

If working from home is what you have always wanted, and it suits your personality and work style, nothing could be better. For others, though, doing a trial run and easing into the work-from-home routine can be the best approach. You may find it isn't all you thought or hoped it would be and decide that being in the office isn't really that bad.

Expense Reimbursement Can Be Expensive

In your position at work, you may only travel occasionally or it may be fairly routine. Before you begin any travel on behalf of your employer, be certain you understand the travel policy as well as expense reimbursement requirements.

Most company travel policies are clear. You may have to use a designated travel agency, and you might be required to have tickets charged to the company's corporate card. Usually the paying credit card is awarded any travel points. Still, having your company pay is generally preferable to charging the expenses on your personal credit card and waiting for reimbursement.

More than likely, you will be expected to travel economically. Unless you are at the executive levels, most organizations won't pay for business or first class. To get the best fare, you may have to settle for a connecting flight or leave at the crack of dawn. If driving, check the mileage reimbursement rate and any restrictions about using your own vehicle.

Usually limits for hotel rooms and for meal reimbursement are specified, but they may vary by location. Some organizations have a per diem rate for food, and receipts may not be required. However, most businesses will want actual receipts for auditing purposes.

Tipping can be a sticky issue. Most policies give guidelines—perhaps 15 percent at restaurants. If you decide you want to tip more, you may have to do so out of your own pocket. The same is true for taxi drivers and hotel staff.

Also, check the policy regarding alcohol. Some organizations cannot, or will not, cover alcohol, even with meals. Fees for in-room snacks, beverages, and entertainment, like movies, almost certainly will be excluded. The hotel room Wi-Fi fee (which can be high) may or may not be covered. Some hotels also charge for gym access which you may have to pay for yourself.

While it might seem like a good travel opportunity, it can be difficult to have a family member accompany you on a business trip. They may be able to stay for free in your hotel room, but most other charges need to be kept separately.

Always keep receipts. A missing receipt may mean reimbursement isn't possible. Submit your reimbursement form as soon after travel as possible. The longer you delay, the more likely you are to misplace receipts. Also, some companies are quite strict about time limits for expense submission.

It may be tempting to pad your reimbursement request, but that is never a good idea. You could receive an inquiry from accounting, or the expenses could be disallowed. At best this makes you look naïve. At worst, it makes you look like you are trying to slide something by and make a few extra dollars. That is not an image you want to project.

Business travel may sound exciting, but as most regular business travelers will tell you, there is frequently some personal cost associated with it. If you don't know your organization's guidelines, travel can be expensive to your reputation as well as to your pocket book.

Crossing Boundaries

How many people hold down more than one job? Some work at two places because they can't find a fulltime job. Others, however, have a fulltime job and do something else in the off hours such as evenings or weekends. These people may have their own consulting business, teach at a college or university, manage or develop websites, or are freelance writers, photographers, or artists.

Sometimes the "extra" occupation may cross boundaries with the fulltime place of employment. For example, you have agreed to teach an evening course at a community college. It was to be held from 6-8pm. Somehow the schedule changed and your class has been rescheduled for 5-7. The problem is that your regular hours for your fulltime job are 9-5. What are your options?

If your workplace has flex hours, you may find your supervisor will agree to your working 8-4. If not, you could try to take vacation time for an hour or two each week for the afternoon of your class. Again, your supervisor may or may not approve your time off.

Other conflicts can occur when an unexpected out-of-town or evening meeting is suddenly scheduled. Your boss is concerned about your main job, and your ability to do it. Anything else is secondary for her.

Sometimes it's tempting to try and insert a task from your secondary job into the work hours of your fulltime job. You use a computer on a regular basis so who would know? Well, the office tech staff might know. And then your boss might know. Remember that any communication or work product using office IT equipment belongs to your employer, and nothing you prepare at work using office capability is considered private. This includes personal correspondence. So, if you need to send a quick text or email, use your own cell phone to do it.

To better understand how your employer views secondary jobs, check the policy manual or employee handbook. You will probably find a policy that addresses these issues. You might also be asked to sign a form describing acceptable internet usage and stating that all work product belongs to your employer. Disregarding these policies can be a serious offense, and you could be reprimanded, or even terminated, if your activity is discovered.

Perhaps even more important are the ethical considerations. You are being paid to do a job. You agreed to work a set number of hours for that job and, ethically, you have an obligation to your primary employer for those hours. Trying to squeeze in work for another employer or for yourself is simply unethical. So think twice before you step over that boundary line.

Nonprofits Are Still Businesses

There is a major misperception that nonprofit organizations and associations are not actual businesses. While they might not be the same as a corporation that manufactures products or sells services for a profit, nonprofits must follow many of the same rules. This includes filing taxes, following state and federal business policies, raising revenue, and managing expenses. The biggest difference is mission versus margin or profit.

Nonprofits are established to carry out certain functions, generally to advance human good, and they must have a charitable or educational mission. Examples of large nonprofits include churches, public schools, and community hospitals, and organizations like the Red Cross, the American Cancer Society, and the YWCA. Every community has a mixture of large and small health and welfare agencies such as homeless shelters, food banks, and mental health services, as well as social advocacy groups that work for human rights and important causes like early childhood education. It is estimated that every year about 30,000 of these nonprofit organizations close their doors. Many fail due to a lack of understanding about good business practices.

Too often, at nonprofits, individuals who work there don't want to be concerned with business issues. They are generally passionate about their cause, dedicated, and hard-working. Frequently, you hear comments such as, "I deliberately chose not to go into business," or, "If I wanted to worry about budgets and finance, I would work at a corporation, not a community agency."

Yet, someone has to manage the business side of nonprofits. As you move up the ladder, you will need to learn at least basic business principles—how to develop and manage a budget, being certain all activities stay within legal and political limits, understanding personnel policies, among others.

So, if the career path you are following is mission driven, find a mentor who will help you learn the business side. Review your employee manual and ask questions regarding how policies were established and how your benefit package was determined. Learn to read basic financial statements. Look at your agency's tax filing (Form 990) that must be made public each year. Ask your supervisor if you can accompany her to some business meetings just for the experience. When the time comes for a promotion to a higher position, being business savvy should give you an edge.

SECTION 10
FOOD FOR THOUGHT

Forget Failure. Learn From Success

In the workplace and in our professional lives, we often agonize about mistakes. Whether large or small, we go over them again and again, trying to understand how we could have misunderstood the situation, the request, or the data, or how we could have been so stupid. We analyze each mistake vowing to learn from it, and promising ourselves not to make that same mistake twice.

We don't look at our successes the same way, but perhaps we should. Are there factors that you can identify and use in future situations to make success more likely? Can you find a common thread that gives you an edge?

Think about what you consider several successful endeavors. Divide each into three parts—planning, implementation, and outcome. Next, find the commonalities and critical factors.

For example, look at your planning efforts. Were you well-prepared? Had you done the necessary homework? Had you gotten advice or data needed to make your argument or explain the benefits of your project? Had you carefully crafted your presentation or pitch? Did you practice what you were going to say? Did you ask a friend or colleague to review your proposal?

Then look at critical decision points. If you laid out the process in advance, did you stick to your script and go through the steps as prepared and practiced? Or, if necessary, were you able to be flexible and just hit the high points? Did you handle questions easily and gracefully with no indication of defensiveness? Were you inclusive and did you give recognition to others as deserved? Did you thank colleagues for their participation without any hint of gloating?

Finally, look at the outcome for each success. Was it exactly what you had been hoping or expecting, or was it only a partial success? If you were given the project go-ahead or the assignment, what came next? How did you go forward? Did you, or can you, build on that success?

If you compare several recent successes, you will be able to recognize an individual success pattern that you can use time and again. Analyze why and how it works and how you can enhance it for even greater success.

It may be useful and necessary to review your mistakes, but you may learn just as much, or more, by looking at your successes.

The Treasure Of Travel

Depending on your life situation and your geographic location, you may have become an experienced traveler at an early age. Perhaps you were lucky enough to spend a semester abroad while in college, or you have vacationed in other countries, or taken a cruise. Maybe, however, you have always wanted to travel but have never been able to do so.

Travel should be more than just a vacation. It should extend your formal education and broaden your perspective. It can provide a better understanding of cultural differences and world conflicts. It can make you more sophisticated and more interesting. It can also make you a more valued employee.

If your job offers the opportunity to travel, take advantage of it as often as you can. No matter what the venue, each travel experience is valuable, whether to another city, another state, or another country.

If you are hoping travel outside the United States might become a reality at work, make sure you are prepared in case it does. Get a passport and keep it current. While you are at it, get a few extra passport pictures in case you need them for a travel visa. Check to see if you will need any special inoculations for certain countries, and, if so, where there is a travel center or health department that offers them. Determine what currency is needed and ask your bank how long it would take to get a small amount of that currency to take with you.

At the same time, look up whether your bank or credit card company charges foreign transaction fees. They can be costly. If possible, get a credit or bank card that does not charge such fees.

Similarly, check with your cell phone carrier or data plan to see what you have to do to use your phone or computer if you are out of the country, and what it costs to do so. Find out how you add an international data plan or get an international calling card.

Go online or buy a travel book that describes the culture and the history of the country you might visit. Check to see if there are special considerations for women travelers regarding clothing or other required customs. For example, in some countries women are expected to cover their heads, arms, or ankles, and drinking alcohol may be forbidden.

Finally, if your company does regular business in another country, try and learn the basics of the language in that country. The more words and phrases you know, the more comfortable you will be in the event you get to visit there.

Keep alert for any travel possibilities at work. Let your manager or boss know that you are interested in traveling, and that you are prepared to do so. Not only will travel add to your life experience and knowledge base, but it will also look good on your annual review and résumé.

Busyness Is Not A Badge Of Honor

There is a school of thought that professionals today put too much stock in the concept of work-life balance. Proponents of this view contend that the focus should simply be on life with a capital "L." There is also some concern that we have entered an era of self-focus (think mani-pedi and massage, gym memberships, and constant connectivity with friends), and that work no longer dominates our lives. Is the average person really working more than forty hours per week, chained to their desks, laptops, and phones? Are people overwhelmed trying to manage their work commitments, or is it that they simply love to complain about being busy so they feel important and needed?

You hear it all the time. You meet someone you haven't seen in a while and you ask how they are doing. How often do they respond that they are overwhelmed, so busy they can hardly keep their head above water? How often is that your response to them?

Then there is the email/text competition. Someone is out of the office for a day or two, and, as soon as they return, they have to announce how many work emails were waiting for them, or how they couldn't enjoy their time off because the text messages never stopped. Counting emails is the adult version of counting Facebook "friends." Just as teens believe Facebook connections are an indication of their popularity, employees equate the number of emails or text messages received with their value in the work setting. Neither can be substantiated as an accurate measure for likeability or worth.

So, is work the culprit, the reason that we can't have balance in our lives? Or is the concept of having "no time" a self-fulfilling prophecy?

A recent American Time Use Survey Summary from the Bureau of Labor Statistics found that employed persons worked an average of 7.6 hours on the job each day. They also found that on an average day, nearly everyone age 15 and over engaged in some sort of leisure activity (5.9 hours for men, 5.2 hours for women). Television and socializing were the major activities. Therefore, in a given work week a person spends about 38 hours working and almost 30 hours in leisure time. When you throw in the weekend, leisure wins hands down. We really can't claim that work is the time eater we all make it out to be. Life activities actually take precedence.

If you feel you do need better time management, there are some steps you can take to begin a correction process. First, be more focused at work so you don't have to take work home with you. Block out periods on your daily calendar for finishing projects and for answering emails or calls. Treat this time as though it were as important as meeting time—because it is.

Learn to say "no" to non-essentials. This includes non-essential meetings, non-essential office gatherings, lunches, or social events you don't enjoy. Protect your time as much as you can.

It might be helpful to do your own time survey. At the end of each work day, take five minutes and list any activities where you wasted work time—that conversation in the lunchroom about a current movie, that fifteen minutes you spent trying to find a flight for the holidays, or that phone call with your sister. Keep track of these non-work activities for an entire week. Do they add up to half an hour a day? An hour? More? Is there a pattern? How can you use your time survey to help you be more productive at work so you have more leisure time after work?

Most importantly, stop wearing busyness as a badge of honor, and stop using it as an excuse for not living your life fully.

Career Paths Are Seldom Linear

Most of us are always looking for direction in our lives, especially our work lives. This search starts in high school when parents, school counselors, friends, and others begin asking what you plan to major in when you go to college. Few high school students can answer this question with clarity. You finally select a college, but it may take a year or two to nail down a major. The sheer number of choices can be overwhelming. Even within a major, there are choices to be made about direction. For example, in business, do you choose accounting or marketing or operations management? In education, you can focus on areas such as pre-k, secondary, or special ed.

The choices may get even more difficult as you start looking for your first professional job. There are so many parameters to consider. Where do you want to live? What type of business or profession is best suited for you? Perhaps most importantly, who will hire you?

Unless a professional path is proscriptive and regimented like becoming a physician or a certified public accountant, it may be difficult to see that linear career path you thought you were on. You may accept one position only to find that you really don't like the field you have chosen. Perhaps you thought you would like sales, or working in a law firm, or in public service, yet find it isn't what you expected or hoped. What now? Do you start over or do you stick it out? Do you go back to school? Do you go back home?

While these questions and their answers are individualistic, there are some general guidelines that might be useful in your current job while you are deciding your future career path. First, whatever your current job, work hard at it. Give it your best effort. You may find that as you become more proficient, you will like it more, or your work may be noticed by a boss and you will be given the additional responsibility you want.

Don't be too hasty about leaving a job. We often second guess our own choices and we are often wrong. It takes time to build experience and competency in a job or field.

Try not to compare your job (or your salary or your life) with those of your friends or your acquaintances on social media. Most people tend to overemphasize their happiness, including their job satisfaction.

Seek out any opportunities your current job offers. If you are invited to attend meetings, training sessions, or conferences, do so. Volunteer for special projects. Meet new people.

Take advantage of any continuing education or certifications available to you. Will your employer pay for a relevant course each year or pay for you to prepare to sit for a licensing exam?

Keep up to date with new developments in your field. Read newsletters, blogs, and journals. Join a relevant professional society or your alumni association. Find a community service project and volunteer.

Make sure you keep your résumé current. Take advantage of networking websites such as LinkedIn. Learn how to use them effectively and professionally.

Don't burn any bridges. Leaving a job well can be just as important as beginning one. Many occupational fields are smaller than you realize, and that boss you dislike now may be the president of your professional association tomorrow.

Most career paths aren't linear. In your work life, you will hold many different jobs, some great, some mediocre. Along the way, you may change direction, refocus, or even start anew. Each of your jobs adds to your experience base. Each employment situation has some opportunity for honing your skills, and for increasing your competency. So take every advantage of the job you have now, even as you prepare for your future career journey.

High Achievers May Not Be The Best Mentors

Sometimes a mentor just seems to materialize. A professor takes an interest in something you have written or a research project you have completed. You find her supportive and encouraging. She is helpful with career advice and is happy to serve as a reference when you are applying for your first professional job.

Other mentors may be found at work. Your first supervisor may help you adjust to the professional workplace and may help you recognize your potential. If you are an engaged employee and perform well at work, this mentor may assist in advancing your career.

These mentors may be "mentors of convenience" or "serendipitous mentors." You didn't seek them out. You were simply lucky to find yourself in their class or in their department at work. Other mentoring relationships, however, must be developed and cultivated. They don't just occur naturally.

Trying to find a mentor can be awkward and intimidating. You generally can't just send someone an email asking them to mentor you. You also can shoot too high, or not high enough, when trying to find a mentor. For example, many people think the best mentor is the most important or the most accomplished person in their organization or field. Often, this is inaccurate. High achievers do not always make good mentors. They may be driven and self-serving, or feel that they are entitled to your adoration. Most likely, they have little time to give to a mentoring relationship, and you can end up feeling like a pest who is encroaching on their time.

To find the right mentor, you need a plan. There are several tips that can help you get noticed and set you up for a productive mentoring relationship. First of all, work hard—harder than all of your colleagues. The best way to get noticed is to have your work ethic stand out.

Volunteer for assignments, but do so strategically. You don't want to be in the basement putting meeting packets together when you could be writing the background introductions of meeting attendees, or assisting a renowned speaker get settled in the meeting room.

Try to attend meetings where possible mentors will be present. Don't attempt to show off at these meetings—that rarely works in your favor. Instead, at the conclusion of the meeting, make an effort to introduce yourself and make a comment or two about some aspect of the meeting content.

Carefully follow the achievements and accomplishments of possible mentors. When you run into one of them in the elevator or at a meeting, you will be prepared to have a meaningful conversation that shows your interest in their area. You also might decide to join a professional society or group in which a desired mentor is active. This will give you additional opportunities to interact with, and impress, the individual.

Not all mentors are alike, and finding the right mentor for you will take some perseverance. What most new professionals need is a mentor who is supportive and thoughtful, one who has vision and who enjoys interacting with various groups and exploring new ideas. When you become more experienced, your mentoring needs will probably change. As you move up the career ladder, you may seek a new mentor who can help you learn and master areas such as business strategies or advanced management techniques.

Most importantly, don't make the mistake of discarding mentors when you feel like you have learned all you can from them. Instead, keep them as valued colleagues. Let them know about your career progress and personal milestones. Send them your new contact information when you change jobs, and always be grateful that they were in your corner.

Male-Entrenched Work Cultures

We frequently hear about how difficult it is for women to reach top leadership positions in corporate America. What we don't often recognize is that many nonprofit organizations also have a male-entrenched leadership culture. For example, in health care women make up 74% of the workforce, but only 18% of hospital CEO positions are filled by women. This isn't a surprising statistic. Even in female-dominated professions, men rise faster through the leadership ranks than women.

Think for a moment about teachers. How often do you still see a divide between female teachers and male principals or administrators? Social workers and nurses are other examples. Over 80% of social workers are women, yet many social service organizations and community agencies have a man at the helm. In nursing, despite, or perhaps because of, the fewer number of men in the profession (around 10%), many male nurses rise quickly to positions of leadership in health care settings.

We hear excuses and explanations for these discrepancies, things like, "Women don't want to leave the classroom," or, "Women make better clinicians, and it would be a waste of talent to put them in an administrator's role." In reality, women make excellent managers, administrators, and CEOs. They bring their classroom and clinical problem solving abilities and a spirit of collaboration and teamwork that transfer nicely from the bedside or classroom to the boardroom.

Why is it so easy to pass over women in favor of men when a top leadership position opens? Partly, it is because "like begets like." Partly, it is because many organizations are male-entrenched. Men are in the top positions and men select the person for the open position. Compounding the problem is that many organizational boards of directors for nonprofits are also predominantly men who seem to have more confidence in male CEOs. Then there are those hard-to-prove gender biases and hidden stereotypes.

The male-dominated workplace is often less hospitable to women. There may be little flexibility for scheduling or working from home, poor maternity leave benefits, or an old boys' network that conducts business at the gym or on the golf course. There may be few women mentors and even fewer examples of women in top positions. These factors can cause a "lack of fit" between a woman, her work world, and her career ladder.

How can these gaps be addressed? If you find yourself in this type of environment, the only option isn't to leave. Instead, be aware of the biases and issues and be sure you don't inadvertently buy into any of the stereotypes. Find a mentor or organizational supporter. If a female mentor isn't available, find a man who can, and will, serve in that role for you. Don't let the environment make you overly cautious or fearful. Instead, volunteer for challenging assignments. Be sure your annual goals and evaluation are based on objective criteria. Learn as much as you can about the organization and its culture, then work to obtain enhanced benefits and flexibility. Finally, find and recommend excellent women candidates for every open position. Even a small number of women in top positions can begin to positively change that male-entrenched culture to one based more on competency and equity.

Beware Of Self-Proclaimed Experts

Perhaps you have tried it a time or two—passing yourself off as an expert and then rushing to become one. Maybe you padded your résumé or job application by slightly overstating your technical expertise or your presentation skills. When your boss asked you to fix a problem or fill in for a speaking engagement, you had to work fast to become as proficient as you had led her to believe you were. In the worst case scenario, you had no choice but to admit your limitations and face the consequences.

There are many self-proclaimed experts in the business world, but they abound in other areas as well. There are life coaches, personal trainers, yoga instructors, financial advisors, event planners, tutors, and others who are self-taught and who lack any formal training or certifications. Some of these individuals may be talented and knowledgeable, but some will not be. Taking their advice may lead to more problems than progress.

With social media, it is easy to present a troubling situation to your circle of friends and ask for their input. It is then tempting to take the consensus opinion and act on that. The problem is that most of your friends may be no more expert in that topic area than you are. No matter how many opinions you gather, opinion does not equate to expertise.

If you are having a serious problem—a problem with your finances, your health or your mental health—seek a qualified professional for advice. These individuals should be licensed and credentialed. Check their background online. Check state licensing boards and consumer groups to see if they have any lawsuits or formal complaints pending against them. Check to see which institutions they are affiliated with, and who else is in the medical practice or financial group. This is simply due diligence. It is a prudent and careful way to move forward in finding needed assistance for a serious problem.

We often ask friends and colleagues to weigh in when we are trying to make a decision. Asking your office mate how they like a certain car, or checking with a coworker about a vacation experience or venue makes sense. Asking them if they think a mole looks suspicious or if a stock purchase is risky makes no sense at all.

The next time a friend asks you for advice, take a moment to decide if you actually have any expertise in the subject area. If you don't, say so. You shouldn't pad your opinion anymore than you should pad your résumé.

Being Responsible For You

Some people dream of being a "free spirit," free of commitments, ties, and responsibilities. Even the phrase "carefree" sounds desirable. For those whose lives are driven by to-do lists, being less scheduled and less burdened seems like an impossibility.

If this picture fits you, it may be time to take stock. You might begin by assessing your actual responsibilities and commitments. Start by making three new lists.

Put real responsibilities on the first list. List one should be fairly easy. It will include your responsibilities for your family, your finances, and your job. These usually are fairly fixed. They make up your "required" responsibilities.

List two should cover any assumed responsibilities. Generally, these commitments and activities are things you have volunteered for, been talked into, or that exist simply by habit. They might include an annual family reunion that creates more stress than pleasure, or a volunteer activity that no longer gives you a feeling of accomplishment. Perhaps it includes a commitment to a monthly event with a friend or colleague that seems to have lost its allure. Also on that list might be weddings that you have been asked to participate in, community events that you may or may not enjoy, or a charitable activity for a cause more important to a colleague than to you. These are "choice" responsibilities. You do them, not because they are required, but because you choose to do them.

The third list may be a bit unusual, but it is equally important. This is a list of your responsibilities to yourself. Commitments to health usually top this list. As an adult, no one is going to nag you about your annual physical and dental check-ups, or getting your flu shot, or taking vitamins. No one but you really cares whether you hit the gym, work too hard, and sleep too little. You are responsible for your own health, your own stress level, and your own happiness. These are huge responsibilities, yet many personal items take a back seat to list one (which may not be avoidable) or list two (which contains numerous avoidable items).

For example, you don't go to the gym on a regular basis because you can't afford the gym membership fees. Yet, the wedding your old college roommate asked you to be a part of (the college roommate you haven't seen in seven years) will require more cash outlay than an annual gym membership and those new contact lenses you need put together.

Or, you thought training for that half marathon your friend talked you into for that charity would be fun. It isn't, and it is a terrible time drain. You've been giving up time with your family in order to do something you don't really enjoy or need to do. In addition, it makes you feel more stressed because of the time pressure.

You get the idea of the tradeoffs you make between lists one, two, and three. It may be difficult to say "no" when you feel flattered by an invitation such as being part of a wedding party, or when asked to spend a week at the beach with your parents and your sister's family (which includes four difficult children). Perhaps you were planning on a quiet "staycation" this year that would let you catch up with things around the house and in your daily life. You were planning to save money this year, rather than springing for high airfares.

Learning to decline unwanted invitations and activities, and saying "no" when things aren't in your own best interest are important skills for being a responsible adult. These actions may take some practice, and every now and then, you may hurt someone's feelings. You may even feel guilty at times, but keep in mind that you have personal obligations, needs, and wants just like everyone else on your lists. Most importantly, only you are responsible for you. That's a big commitment.

Career Success Is Self-Defined

It's surprising how everyone wants to be successful, yet few people have a clear definition of what success means for them. Many equate success with money. Others equate it with fame or power. Still others see it as achieving a long life, being happy, or bringing about positive social change. Some see it as finding a life partner and having a family. Others have a narrower focus like owning a home or being able to retire or to travel.

The beauty of success is that it's self-defined. Whether in the workplace or the world, success is individually determined.

Defining success in one's career can be difficult and elusive. For some, success in business means becoming the boss or CEO. Others see it as owning the company or business. Still others see a six-figure or higher salary as the measure of true career success.

What many people new to the professional workforce don't realize is that there are numerous critical components of success. You need a vision, clear goals, perseverance, and a tolerance for risk and failure. Most likely there will be setbacks and deviations, perhaps even a course correction. Two other important success characteristics are belief in yourself and self-confidence.

A career, from first job to retirement, can span over 40 years. If you spend five years in each job, you might work in eight or more organizations. If you change jobs more frequently, you could work for a dozen or two dozen employers. In each new job or new position you have a new opportunity to redefine success not only as it relates to that particular job, but also as it relates to your long-term vision of success.

As you move through your career, remember that only you can define what success means for you, and only you can achieve that success.

Giving Back

For decades, women have been helping other women move forward in their educational pursuits and in their careers. From assistance like babysitting co-ops in the 60s to current online leadership coaching, women have recognized how difficult it can be to get ahead professionally. As a result, today there is a growing commitment on the part of many women to provide support and encouragement.

We have seen the growth of foundations and programs that help women recognize their value, help young mothers finish their high school and college degrees, and help women enter male-dominated careers. We have watched more women run large and small businesses, sit on corporate boards, and be elected to important political positions. Many of these women leaders have written useful books that detail their struggles and paths to success. Almost always, their narratives include mention of mentoring and support from other women.

Even as a relatively new professional, you are now in a position to give back and to help other women succeed. Something as simple as reviewing a résumé and cover letter, or helping someone upload her information for a job website can go a long way. Other easy, but positive, activities include discussing possible job interview questions and answers, or giving some advice about professional dress and demeanor with a young woman who is going on a job interview.

You might offer to participate in programs for women at the local high school or community college, or at local events that help and encourage women to enter the professional workforce. Programs targeting women always need help with their projects and fundraising efforts. Your input, assistance, and donations will be appreciated.

As you move up the career ladder, you will have many opportunities to serve as a mentor or coach for women just starting their careers. When you are approached for assistance, take a few minutes to think about all of the women who helped you succeed. Then decide if it is your turn to give back.

ABOUT THE AUTHORS

Elizabeth (Betsy) Clark, PhD, is the President and Co-Founder of Start Smart Career Center. She is an experienced CEO and national leader who has held executive positions in health care, nonprofit organizations, and academia. A lifelong advocate for women's rights and economic equality, she serves on numerous boards of directors of cause-related or professional associations, and is a champion for increasing the number of women in board leadership positions. Her current emphasis is on mentoring young women for workplace success and career advancement.

With degrees in social work, public health, and medical sociology, Betsy is a recognized expert, author, and speaker on the topics of cancer, hope, loss and grief. She has traveled extensively and has a particular interest in hospice and palliative care in underserved countries. She and her husband love the mountains and live in the Catskill Mountain region of New York. They have three children and four grandchildren.

Elizabeth F. Hoffler, MSW, is the Executive Director and Co-Founder of Start Smart Career Center. She is a healthcare social worker with a focus on public policy and advocacy who has advanced quickly from entry level jobs to positions of leadership and management in national nonprofit organizations. She attributes much of her success to having strong women mentors who pushed her to take advantage of every opportunity and accomplish her professional goals no matter the obstacles.

In addition to her work in nonprofits, Elizabeth is also a PhD student and is focusing her studies on underserved and vulnerable populations, and finding innovative, policy-oriented solutions to some of society's most pressing problems. Elizabeth lives outside of Washington, DC with her husband and two pugs, Bubbles and Bonkers.

www.ingramcontent.com/pod-product-compliance
Lightning Source LLC
Chambersburg PA
CBHW061646040426
42446CB00010B/1610